Table of Contents

Introduction

There are a ton of reasons why somebody would want to start a vegetable garden, which range from finances to health and from the environmental impact to the mental benefits.

It's Organic (and Tastier!)

The problem is that users of chemicals in the production of vegetables to meet demand are not very healthy for humans to eat. Our bodies weren't designed to be pumped full of strange chemicals. Growing your vegetables with an organic approach removes these harmful chemicals from the equation so that you don't find yourself consuming poison or carcinogenic toxins. This makes growing your own vegetables a healthy choice, though it is far from the only reason it is healthier.

It's Cheaper

The best way to lower the cost of the vegetables in your diet is to grow them yourself. You will need to invest a little money up front and throughout the growing process, but this investment will pay for itself quickly as your grocery bill shrinks. The most cost-effective way to have fresh vegetables is to cut out all the middlemen and grow your own.

But while we're on the topic of money…

Make Money With a Vegetable Garden

If you are growing vegetables in your garden anyway, then adding a couple more with the intent to sell what they produce can be a great way to earn back your initial investment If you take those same vegetables and sell them, you can earn back that investment with extra to cover the interest.

You Eat Healthier and More Creatively When You Have a Vegetable Garden

When they start growing their own vegetables, most beginners are surprised at how much they can harvest. These nutritious plants end up in all sorts of different meals, if for no other reason than the fact that they need to be used (or preserved) before they can go bad.

When you have tons of them from a good harvest, you will find yourself getting creative with your meals. There are thousands of new recipes to be found on the internet every day, and it is much less risky to ruin a few carrots when you have tons, unlike when you buy them from the store.

It's Better for the Environment

Starting your own vegetable garden is more impactful in reducing the number of fossil fuels that are burnt as part of your eating. When you go to the grocery store and purchase vegetables, you are also paying for the gas that was required to move that vegetable across the country. By growing your own vegetables, you create food without having to burn fossil fuels, which reduces your carbon footprint. If you sell those vegetables locally, then you can reduce the number of vegetables that need to be shipped into your local area, which means that you are also helping to reduce the carbon footprint of your community this way.

Growing Your Own Vegetables is Great Exercise

One way that thousands of people across the world get their exercise is through working in their gardens. Despite often being down on your hands and knees, vegetable gardening is a great way to get exercise, and this is just another of the many ways that starting a vegetable garden is an investment in your health.

Soil needs to be mixed and moved around the yard. You need to get down to the plant level and then up to your feet again. It gets you outdoors in the natural sunlight, which is a natural antidepressant, and the fresh air, which makes the lungs happy. Gardening helps in releasing endorphins the brain, which makes one happier while the exercise keeps you in good health. So instead of paying for a monthly gym pass, you can get your exercise while growing a crop that will pay you instead.

Grow a Variety of Foods

Most vegetable gardens are full of staples; lettuce and carrots, potatoes and tomatoes, pumpkins and peppers are common. You are free to grow one of these or all of them as you see fit, and this offers plenty of variety. It doesn't need to be carrots for dinner every night, your options are only limited by what you decide to grow.

The fact of the matter is that there are thousands of possibilities for what you can grow in your vegetable garden. Not only are there going to be all sorts of vegetables that will work perfectly, but also, this number grows exponentially when you take into account the many subspecies there are. For example, tomatoes can be fist-sized, or you can choose to grow cherry tomatoes instead.

Chapter 1- Siting your Own Vegetable Garden

If we are going to be starting a vegetable garden, then the very first thing that we need to do is pick a location for our vegetable garden. In your backyard, there are dozens of places in which you could plant your garden depending on how you space it or position it, and also the size of your backyard. Each possibility is technically in your backyard, but locations aren't all made the same. Some are better than others, and some are downright unsuitable for gardening.

In this stage of your planning, you should take a moment to consider each of the following environmental attributes. Some of these you can tell just by looking at your yard, but others will require a little bit of data gathering. These steps are included where necessary. You can get by with growing in a location that is a little less than ideal for some of these attributes, but spots which fail on multiple fronts are best avoided.

Elevation: This one can usually be done through eyesight alone. Looking at the space you are thinking about planting your vegetables, is it elevated? Is it on an incline? Is it at the bottom of an incline? Is it rather flat? Depending on which of these questions is the most accurate, you are going to have a unique relationship to watering your plants. Generalized advice on watering your plants assumes that they are in a flat space. Plants that are on an incline will act flat. Plants on the bottom of an incline are going to need less water. Those planted on an elevated surface will require more water than normal.

Sunlight: Plants need a certain amount of sunlight a day. Some species prefer this light to be direct. Others prefer it to be indirect, in the shade. Some want as much sun as possible, while others need relatively little direct sunlight. If you are going to be growing vegetables, then you are going to need to know two things. You are going to need to research the species of plant to see how much sunlight it needs, and you are going to need to know how much sun your chosen space gets. Keep an eye on the space throughout a day and see how much time it is in the sun and in the shade. Finding this out will let you know which vegetables will do the best in this particular space. If you are looking to plant some veggies that want a lot of suns and some that don't want much, then remember that you don't need to grow everything in the same bed. It is better to grow multiple beds than try to force a plant out of its comfort zone.

Coverage: How much foliage or coverage from rain and wind does space have? Are plants going to be safe from high winds where you plant them? Are they going to be able to get enough water when it rains, or is the foliage going to misdirect it? Flipside, is the foliage going to help to prevent drier plants from drowning? Coverage isn't necessary when it comes to vegetable gardening, but many gardeners have no choice but to work with it because of having trees in their backyards or limited space.

Security: How safe are your vegetables? Vegetable farming doesn't tend to bring out thieves the same way that cannabis or fruit farming does. Well, at least not human thieves. Vegetable farming does bring out mice, rabbits, deer and other herbivores. While seeing a deer eating your vegetables is a good sign (after all, it means they must be pretty tasty), it also means that you now have a half-ruined crop. If there is easy access to your backyard or growing space, then you should consider how you can add some security to prevent unwanted visitors. This can be as easy as adding a knee level plastic fence around the garden. Still, if you can offer security in one direction (such as when growing next to a house), then you can save money by using less fencing and limiting critters from approaching.

Ease of Access: This is the one factor that causes the most problems, but new gardeners don't realize it until it is too late. When you are first planning out your garden, it is easy to forget about the fact that you are going to need to be able to maneuver through it. Maintaining your crops requires you to water each plant and inspect it for signs of problems. If you plant your crops in such a way that you can't get easy access to some of them, then you are going to end up neglecting those plants, and they will reflect this in their yield. Most gardeners get a pack of vegetable seeds and then plant them too close together. When the plant you are growing is so tiny, to begin with, it is easy to forget what size they are going to be growing too. This is the reason that crops are most often planted in rows. Try to keep size in mind and ensure that there is enough space for you not only to get at every plant but to be able to get down and inspect each one.

Ground or Container: The majority of this manual is written under the assumption that you are growing your plants in the ground itself. At this stage, it is important to note that, while there are some general differences between these two methods, there are also many similarities. Whether you are growing containers that are above ground or below ground, they tend to need to be watered more often than plants grown outside of a container. Beyond this main difference, they will still require as much sunlight, security and ease of access as any other garden bed you plant.

Putting It All Together: Once you have considered each of these attributes of the space, you can decide if it will be a good fit for your plants or not, as determined by their needs. Figuring out each of these attributes will take time and make it a long wait before you are ready to plant your vegetables, but it can save you from some nasty surprises that could lead to weak veggies and poor yield. A spot that looks perfect at first glance might not get enough sunlight or shade for the plants you were looking to put there. Knowing this ahead of time allows you to match your garden to the local conditions so you can have the most productive vegetable garden possible.

Chapter 2-   Planning and Designing Your Garden

Now we're onto the fun part of planning. We can start to imagine what delicious veggies we are going to be eating soon. It's time to get back to the old drawing board, as now you are going to decide the layout of your particular garden. Again, grab a pen and some paper, then get your ruler and get down to business.

As with the layout of your yard, you are going to mark on the paper specific lengths, as well as how far each length represents. I once again recommend that you use inches and that you cover your entire garden space. By now, you should know which plants you wish to plant in your garden, so once again, you must look at the needs of each of these plants, then plan to put them in the ground accordingly.

Some plants require more space than others, which means that while you can still have them in your garden, you do need to place them carefully to ensure they all fit. Lettuce and radishes, for example, can be planted close together and still do fine.

Tomatoes and peppers, on the other hand, require more space – you won't be able to plant as many of these in your garden as the others.

Again, you can play around with different designs until you find what works for you. Remember to plant them based on their growing preferences, and to place them in the garden for optimal growth.

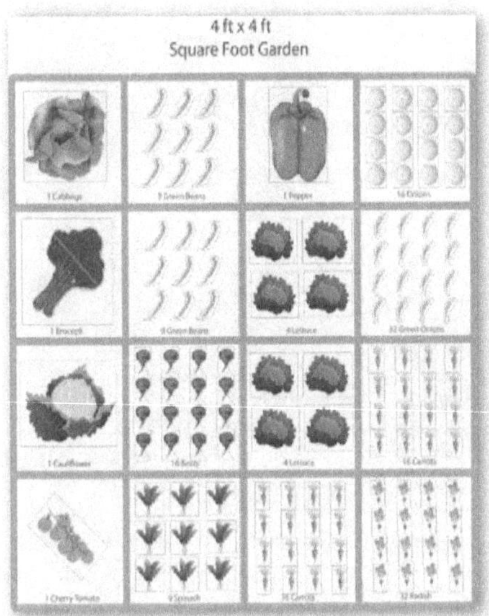

Some gardeners choose to simply plant the plants they like, and place them into the garden where they fit. Other gardeners prefer to be highly systematic with their gardens, and end up planting what looks like puzzles in the ground.

If you choose to plant this way, you do have the opportunity to turn your garden into a work of art as well as a source of food. Take a look at the diagram and see how this gardener planned to place their herbs and veggies.

Not only will the plants do well if they are placed this way, but the colors will complement each other as they grow, making the garden visually appealing as well as a source of food.

Now, some feel that to get a good idea of how your garden is going to look, you will have to take the time to study it over several years with a trial and error method. However, with a simple trick, you can actually get an idea of how your garden will look without having to wait at all.

Grab your list of plants, then get online and find images of them. Scale down the images, then print them out. Cut out as many images as you are going to plant in your garden, then piece them together on the table in front of you.

If you don't want to use actual images, simply use the colors each plant will

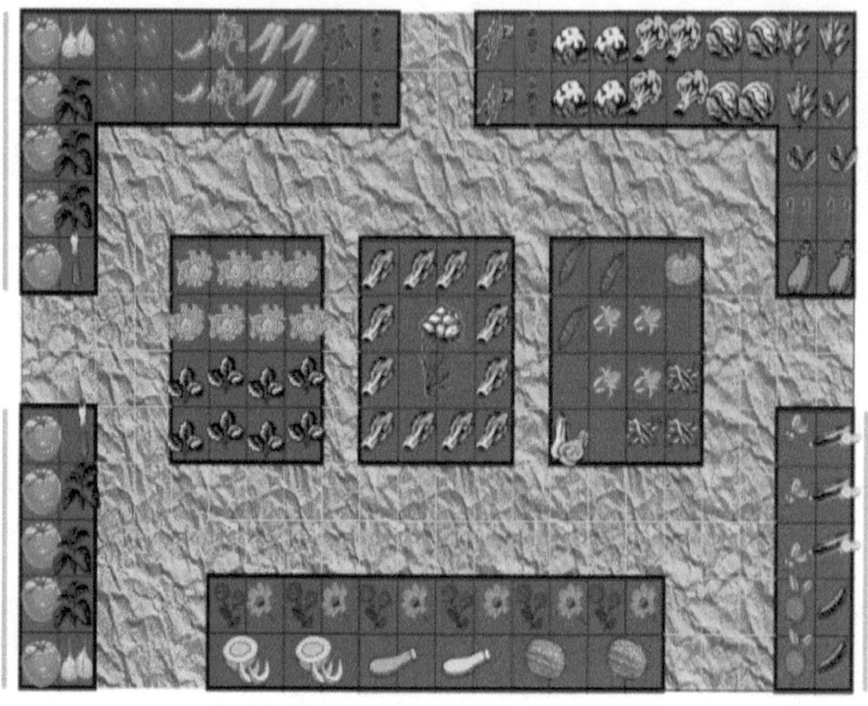

be and give yourself an idea of what your grown garden will look like.

Depending on the size of your garden, you may need to make paths in between to reach all the different species. Make sure you factor this into your garden diagram, so you know how the overall look of the garden will be. Again, you can do this using both the garden plan itself, as well as the layout plan you used for your yard. Combine this with the visual of the colors, and you can give yourself an incredibly accurate idea of what your garden is going to look like when it's completed.

Don't be afraid to mix and match the plants you put into your garden, either. It's all just a matter of planning.

As with the vegetable gardening, you can plan the final look of your garden in advance using images of the flowers or simply using their colors. However, flowers tend to grow vastly different than vegetables, and you will need to compensate for their different needs.

The giant sunflower, for example, can reach a height of over 6 feet and can grow incredibly thick stalks. While this is beautiful to see, the fully grown plants can potentially hide the sun from the smaller plants that didn't grow as tall – which will pose a problem if those other plants need a lot of sunlight.

On the other hand, you can use this to your advantage. Sunflowers, for example, require a lot of sun in the day while strawberries can handle partial shade. If you plan carefully, you can plant the taller plants in such a way that they will give enough shade for the plants that don't require as much sun.

This will require you to do more research in the beginning, but as you can see, all this preparation is going to pay off when you have your plants in the ground. A square foot gardener understands the need to plan and is willing to put in the time and effort to write it down.

The more experienced you become, the less you will have to do this, but in the beginning, it's crucial you know what you are putting into the ground, and where. Trust me, take the time to do this now, and when your garden is in the ground, you can rest easy, knowing that it's going to grow well and how you wanted.

That's really all you need to get your square foot garden started. After you have your plants in the ground, you cross over into the realm of maintenance. Water the plants according to the recommendation for the variety, and remember always to soften the flow of water into the garden.

Once the plants have become established and start to grow, weed the garden regularly. Remember, the time and effort you put into it are going to directly affect the produce and flowers you get out of it.

It is better to plant multiple garden beds for plants with different needs. You will know exactly how much space you have to work with and what conditions you can give your veggies. Use this to decide what to plant and which spot it should be in. You can grow anything you want, just research its needs ahead of time so that you know in which space to put it and how to keep it healthy

Summarized Step-by-step Guide

List the crops you want to grow. Divide this list into two categories: must-grow and would like to grow.

1. For each plant, decide whether you want to start seeds indoors, purchase transplants, or direct sow.

2. Based on your decisions, write down the planting date for each crop. To do this, first, find your average last frost date and use the plant timing instructions.

3. Note the harvest category of each crop. Place a star beside any plants with a quick-burst or weather-dependent harvest; they are prime candidates for succession planting.

4. For each plant, look up the recommended plant spacing. Then decide how many plants (or how many rows) you will plant for each crop.

5. List any companion planting combinations you want to incorporate.

6. Brainstorm any vertical gardening ideas you want to try (see here).

7. For raised or in-ground beds, draw a layout grid of your garden space (graph paper is a great help). Each square represents 1 foot. If you're growing in containers, sketch out a top view of each container. If the container is circular, draw a square inside, noting the distance between the sides of the square.

8. In your layout, use a pencil to sketch in your must-grow crops. Then fill any remaining space with the crops you would like to grow. For the crops with a star, decide how you will use succession planting in those spaces. Some areas may have two crops listed if you plan to plant a second crop after the harvest of the first one.

9. Now that your garden layout is taking shape to adjust it as necessary. You may decide to add more containers or change the quantities of crops.

10. With your rough plan in place (don't worry, you can still change it!), it's time to start building your garden.

Chapter 3-   Different Types Of Gardens

What do you envision when you think of a vegetable garden? Vegetables in neat, uniform rows in a dedicated plot of land? Let's explore the different types of gardens you can design which best suits your needs and skills.

Container Gardening

In a container garden, vegetables and herbs grow in a limited space, such as a pot or large planter. Many beginners enjoy container gardens because the labor involved is minimal. You don't have to prepare the ground, and weeding is almost nonexistent. You can also place your pots in the best location for the plants you're growing.

But container gardening isn't free of challenges. The cost of the containers and soil can add up. Plants in containers require great attention to watering, and in the heat of summer may need watering several times per day. Container plants also need more fertilization, because the continual watering leaches away nutrients and the plants cannot access nutrients in the ground soil.

With proper attention and care, however, container gardens are rewarding. Great options for container growth include lettuce, greens, snap peas, peppers, tomatoes, and herbs.

Raised Bed Gardening

Raised beds combine the best features of in-ground and container gardens. Like containers, with proper mulching, you won't need to weed as often. But unlike containers, the plants' ability to send their roots into the native soil to access water and nutrients cuts down on both watering and fertilizing. Raised bed gardens, when done right, are very attractive. (Many people build raised beds on top of a solid surface such as paved ground. This design acts more like a container garden in terms of soil, water, fertilization, and drainage requirements.)

The biggest downside to raised beds is the initial cost and labor. You also cannot easily move them if you change your mind about the ideal location. Predesigned kits available at garden centers make the labor barrier easier to overcome.

Most gardeners who choose raised beds find the trade-offs to be worth it both in time saved over the season and their overall gardening experience. Almost all crops grow well in raised beds; some popular ones include tomatoes, beans, broccoli, peppers, onions, and zucchini.

Vertical Gardening

Whether you choose an in-ground garden, a container garden, a raised bed garden, or a combination of all three, consider adding vertical gardening to your plan.

When you train vining plants on a trellis, you make space for more crops in the container or bed. Plus, the better airflow achieved with vertical gardening reduces the risk of many common plant diseases.

Exercise your creative side: You can use free materials such as gathered sticks to build a trellis or make a small investment in a cattle-panel arch trellis. Sturdy trellises can last for many seasons.

Great crops for vertical gardening include pole beans, climbing peas, cucumbers, and even melons.

Rows

This is the most common and basic plan for a layout. Vegetables are planted in long, straight rows, orientated in a north to south direction. This orientation ensures the most exposure to sunlight, as well as the best air circulation for your plants. Plants growing in rows running east-west will throw shadows onto the neighboring crops or be in the shade of the rows next to them. Remember that your vegetable plants need sun all day long.

Tall plants like beans or corn should be planted on the northern side so that they do not shade the smaller crops. Plant medium-high vegetables like cabbage, squash and tomatoes in the center of your patch and reserve the south side for the smaller plants like radishes, lettuce and carrots. How many rows you make will depend entirely on the number of plants you intend to grow. This layout is ideal for people with a lot of gardening space.

Square Foot

At first glance, this layout looks much like the previous one. There is a difference, though. Your squares will now each be one foot by one foot. Each one will again be divided into smaller squares, leaving you with sixteen squares. Use string or wood attached to the frame to make a grid. This will help you once you start planting. Each section will contain the same type of veggie. The grid will help you to separate the different types of vegetable plants.

You have to calculate how many plants you can grow in each section. This will depend on the space each plant needs. Carrots, for example, need around three inches. Divide your square foot bed into three, and you have the answer of four. You can, therefore, divide your square foot section into four by four smaller plots and plant a total of sixteen carrot plants in it. Beans need more space, so plant only four per section.

All vine type plants should be planted at the back of the garden to allow space for their trellises.

Chapter 4-   Essentials Garden Tools

Gardening can be done in several ways, but if you have chosen a container garden, you should have specific gardening tools for you to succeed. If you intend to acquire the most substantial part of your crops, you need to begin the planning before time. Purchase your seeds and garden equipment so that there will be time to sprout and germinate seeds.

Numerous gardening tools could be purchased, but the following are the essential tools for container gardening:

1. Small shovel

A small shovel is perfect for pots. It makes it simple to dig in fertilizers and also to plant your crops or seeds in the pot.

2. Hand Weeder

A hand weeder is a small fork class of tools with a long neck. It's useful for planting seeds and small plants and removing the little weeds that grow in containers. It can be used to dig a tiny hole to put the plant or seed.

3. Plant containers

A plant container is a container for the crops, and it has to be the right size. You can make use of any container for growing plants and vegetable crops. Wooded boxes or crates, gallon-sized coffee cans, old washtubs, as well as five-gallon buckets can be used for growing vegetables in as much as there is sufficient drainage.

4. Small cups or egg cartons to start seeds:

You can use this for sprouting seeds. Ascertain your container is sufficiently broad to give room for the seeds to germinate. If you do not have enough space, the plants have to be transplanted as they grow. Also, you may need to buy a seed heating device as most times you a required to sprout them within, for it to be adequately warm so that they can germinate and grow.

5. Soil

Quality potting soil is a determinant for your plants to grow well. That is the secret to a successful container garden. If you use poor soil, your plants or seeds will not grow. The soil means a lot. Make sure you get top quality soil that your plants require to thrive with or without fertilizer.

6. Plant seeds:

A plant seed can be flower or vegetable seeds. The ideal thing is to look for high-quality seeds if you are to plant vegetables to be able to harvest seeds and keep for another season. Determinate tomatoes and shrub type plants grow brilliantly well in containers. If you're looking forward to the best crops in your pots, go for these types of plants.

7. Garden Gloves:

Though garden glove may not be very essential if you are the type that easily got disgusted by dirt and didn't want stain beneath your nails, or sensitive to some particular plants, you need garden gloves. Also, if you do not want to lay your hand on a caterpillar, tomato hornworm, snail and gardens insects when removing them from your favorite crops, garden gloves do the job better. It will also guard your hands against thorns or all other sharp components of the plants.

8. Watering can:

Watering can do the job better by making the task of watering plants simple and trouble-free because water is running out of it in the form of trickling rain. You can, however, make use of a milk jug to convey water outside. But if you are to use it, ensure you gently pour the water in your hand and spread with your fingers to enable the water to scatter and drop softly into the soil. If not, water coming from jug may land heavily on the soil and splashback on the crop's foliage, raising its danger of having fungus issues and other infections.

9. Trowel:

A trowel is also an essential tool for container gardening. It is being used to loosen up compressed dirt as well as digging through trash in plant containers. Rather than using your hands, the trowel will get the task done better and faster and leave your hand dirt free.

10. Pruners:

A pruner is useful for cutting off dead foliage and pruning plants. Though you might think of using scissors, it is not advisable to use it. There are wet saps on plants that may leave remains stick and rust on your scissors. Cutting plants with scissors instead of pruner also increase the risk of the plants being infected. Pruner is more active in cutting thicker crop stems, also enable clean cut while leaving your plants healthier in the containers.

11. Plant Organic Pesticide:

If you are a non-fastidious type who could squish insects and not have a bad feeling, a pesticide may not be necessary for you. However, if the reverse is the case, it is ideal you have a plant-safe pesticide as part of your tools. Ensure you adhere to all instructions on its usage because it may not be right on food plants. Possibly, you can remove the pest from the plants and spray them on the floor with the pesticide.

12. Stick or String:

These are essential for supporting container plants that needed to be upheld. An example is tomato plants (string and stick or tomato cage can be used to support tomatoes). They can also be used for young trees that needed to be upheld to grow in a straight line up and plants growing up the fence. Stick can be bought at your local garden store. String or yarn could be an organic color, like brown or dark green, for it not to stand out in the garden environment.

13. Quality Fertilizer:

Fertilizer is also essential for the growth of your plant. Having secured good soil, ensure you obtain a high-quality organic fertilizer to get the best result from crops. Compost can be in pellet or liquid form. You can buy specific fertilizer for each type of your plants like rose or citrus fertilizer. However, an all-purpose plant fertilizer does the job for most gardeners. Compost can as well be used to supplement your crop's feeding

14. Potting Bench:

A potting bench is also an essential tool for gardeners. Firstly, it serves as a platform to assemble and store your small appliances, plant marker, fertilizer, and the likes. You can also use it to conveniently move your planting tools from one place to another (for example, from your kitchen to your garden)

Each of the gardening tools is very important for your container garden to be successful. Make sure to have them at your disposal to ease work as well as getting the best results out of your products.

Chapter 5-   Preparing your Vegetable Garden

Clearing Your Garden Spot

The first step is cleaning up space so the soil will not be hard to work on. One can clear your garden space any time of the year, but the most optimal is the season before you plant.

1. Outlining the spaces of your garden plot where clearing is needed.

Outlining the areas depend on how you want the plots to be shaped. Try to follow these straightforward guidelines:

If you want the edges of a rectangular or square plot straight, stretch a cord in between the marked line and sticks with white limestone that is ground, which is easily accessible at garden stores.

If you are seeking a circular garden, utilize a rope or hose to outline the area, and ensure that you are fixing the stature to create a leveled curve.

2. Start by clearing the surface. To do this, you will be razing the plants, bushes, weeds, and rocks. Use a mower if you want to cut the weeds and grass near the surface.

3. Dig out the roots of tough weeds and small tress using a hoe, shovel, or pickaxe.

Killing Weeds and Aggressive Grasses

Weeds are the bane of beautiful gardens. Even when you have cultivated a proper garden, you need must weed it from time to time. Be that as it may, weeding is especially important when you are preparing your garden for the first time.

When preparing a garden, you must get rid of the grass and the weeds as much as possible. Depending on the size of the garden, this process can take quite some time to complete.

You can eliminate weeds and active grasses using two ways described below:

Sifting and Digging by hand: In the case of a minute garden digging up the entire earth and cautiously sifting the soil must be done. Carefully remove root and sod parts that might grow up the following year as weeds.

Put a Covering: An easy and chemical-free technique to clear your garden is to cover it with cardboard, clear or black plastic, even old rugs. The existing plants cannot stand these drastic conditions, such as lacking light from the sun and energy, so they eventually die after a month or so.

The plastic rolls can be bought from the home improvement centers and hardware stores. It is necessary that you use the thickest cardboard or plastic. Controlling weeds and grasses by applying covering to your garden spot is straightforward if you follow these steps:

Spread the covering over your entire garden spot, safeguarding the edges with auxiliary rocks, boards, or bricks.

After a month, remove the covers and cut off any grass or weeds with the aid of a shovel. Try to cut at the root level (just underneath the soil surface). If they aren't too thick, rototiller can be employed.

Analyzing and Improving Your Soil

After you have cleared your garden, the next major step is to have a close look at your soil; give it a hard squeeze, have it checked and tested, improve it, and then work it out to ensure that it is in good shape. Healthy soil gives vegetable roots a balance of all the things they require viz. moisture, air, and nutrients. If you know your soil type, it enables you to neutralize problems that you may face when working on your piece of land.

Testing your soil

Vegetables are kind of fussy about soil chemistry. Excess of a particular nutrient or lacks of a particular nutrient, and you have complications.

The quality of the soil is pivotal to the health of the plants. While testing the soil, you need to check for its pH value and make the necessary amendments. You also need to check the drainage of your soil. To do so, you should soak the soil by hosing it down. Let the area remain undisturbed for a day. The next day, take a handful of the soil and squeeze it hard. If you find that water is streaming out of your hand, it means that the drainage of the soil is poor. You should add organic matter or compost for better drainage. Alternatively, you may want to invest in raised beds.

Now, you should check the soil by opening your hand. If you find that the soil has not balled up or the ball breaks down at the slightest touch, the soil may be too sandy. On the other hand, the ball may not break down even if it is poked hard. This denotes that the clay content is high. In both of these cases, you should be adding organic matter. This will improve the texture of the soil and make it suitable for the growth of the plants.

If the ball breaks down when poked, the conditions of the soil are just perfect for plant growth. This is the property of loam soil.

The exact pH enables vegetables to utilize nutrients from the soil. If your soil's pH is not within the specified range, plants can take up the nutrients such as phosphorus and potassium even if they are abundant in the soil. On the other hand, the solubility of certain minerals like manganese may increase to toxic levels if the pH is extremely low.

Most vegetables prefer a slightly acidic environment (pH ranging between 6 and 7) for their optimal growth.

The only way to assess whether your soil is fit for your vegetables is to test it. Don't panic, analyzing your soil is not complex. Here are the two methods to test your soil:

Use a do it yourself kit: If you want to access the acidity or alkalinity of your soil, the basic pH test kit can be utilized, available at a nursery. This kit can sometimes assist in calculating the major nutrient content. However, the test only gives you a rough estimate of the pH and nutrient levels in your soil.

Contact a soil lab do a test for you: A comprehensive soil test might turn out to be a good investment as a soil lab can thoroughly examine your soil. Soil labs don't charge you a lot. Your local Cooperative Extension Service office or private lab can conduct a comprehensive and reliable soil test. It gives you further insight into your soil; here is what you will know in addition to the pH level:

Since we have seen how to analyze the soil, we will now turn our attention to ways of improving the soil.

To grow plants properly, you need to ensure that the soil is the right one for it. Most plants need the soil of neutral pH, but some tend to require alkaline or acidic soils. Whatever be the type of soil you have, it is possible to modify it so that it becomes more suitable for the plant you wish to grow. However, the steps you take will not have an everlasting effect. Unless you are planning to undertake the steps regularly, you should try using the soil that you have.

Adjusting soil pH

To increase the alkalinity of the soil, you can add ground lime. For increasing the acidity, you can use Sulphur or aluminum Sulphate. All Cooperative Extension Service offices, various lawn and garden centers, and many soil labs have charts showing the quantity of lime and sulfur to be added to fix the pH imbalance. You first have to measure the area of your vegetable garden; the chart tells you the quantity in pounds to be added per 1,000 square feet.

Increasing the Soil's Nutrient Content

If you discover that your soil has a low amount of nutrients, you should add some organic matter to it. Manure and compost can enrich the soil while improving its texture. You can also use organic mulches such as deciduous leaves, straw, and dried grass clippings. These mulches can break down and provide the soil with organic nutrients and improve the soil structure at the same time.

Perfect loam soil is rare, so don't worry if you are deprived of it. To fix your grimy clay or loose sand, you need to add organic matter. You can't change your type of soil altogether, but supplementing organic matter makes your soil more like loam, which is impeccable for vegetable roots. Even if you are lucky enough to have loam soil, adding organic matter to your soil every year will further increase productivity.

Organic matter improves the garden soil as it assists loosening and provides proper ventilation to clay soil. It enhances the water and nutrient holding capacity of sandy soil.

Organic matter attracts vital microorganisms, beneficial fungi, worms, and other soil-borne organisms that enhance the health of your vegetables.

Mulching

The importance of mulching should never be underestimated. It can insulate the soil and thereby keep the roots of plants safe from extremes in temperature. It can also enable the roots to remain moist by retaining water. More importantly, mulching can curb the growth of weeds in your garden.

Various kinds of mulch can be used. You can purchase a range of them at stores. Some of them are specially created to solve certain specific issues in a garden. However, for general purposes, you can easily make mulch at home.

You simply need to gather all dead organic matter in your gardens, such as dead leaves and broken branches. Your garden itself will yield enough plant matter for use as mulch. Collect this organic matter throughout the year in a designated area and break them down into small particles with machines or by hand. Let the mulch remain all winter. The following spring, you will have enough mulch for use in your garden.

Composting

Compost is regarded as the best organic material to supplement your soil. Composting simply breaks down the waste material into a brittle soil-like material called humus. It is easily accessible and pretty straightforward to use.

Compost is basically decayed organic matter. It acts as a natural fertilizer for your garden. It can be an excellent addition to all kinds of soils. You can easily purchase compost at a low cost, even in bulk amounts. On the other hand, you can make your own compost at home for the garden.

There are many other organic matters such as sawdust and manure that can be employed, but compost has surpassed all these organic matters. Using other organic matters except compost can cause problems. For instance, sawdust undoubtedly adds value to your soil upon converting into humus, but when it decomposes, it deprives the soil of nitrogen. It gives rise to the problem of adding more fertilizer to compensate for the effect. In case you are using livestock mature, it will replenish the nitrogen level of the soil, but the abnormal growth of weeds can be observed as livestock diet consists of abundant hay that contains plenty of weed seeds.

It is always good to use fully composted organic matter; that is prepared for a year or two, so it is decomposed completely, and the salts are drained off properly. Too much salt in the soil can be detrimental to plants. Good quality compost and completely decomposed manure should have a dark brown appearance, earthy odor, and have minute original material evident.

Chapter 6-   Seeds and Transplants

When you start your container garden, you can either choose to start your plants off from seed or to buy seedlings and transplant them. There are pros and cons to these two approaches, and it depends on several factors as to which you choose.

Availability

The big advantage of seeds is that there are many more varieties available than seedlings. There are hundreds of varieties of tomato seed, yet you will only ever find a half dozen, if that, varieties of tomato seedling in the stores. Some of the best-tasting vegetables are only available as seeds, so you need to decide what you want to grow.

Planting Time

If you have left it too late in the growing season to start plants from seeds, then you are going to have to buy seedlings. I grow a lot of my plants from seed, but usually a month or two into the growing season, I realize I have some space or some seedlings haven't germinated, so I usually end up buying some seedlings too. If you are a little too late to get the seeds in, then buy some seedlings, your choice of variety will be limited, but at least you will get the plants in!

Germination Time

Some seeds take a long time to germinate or are hard to germinate. These can be started off yourself from seed, or you may choose to buy seedlings purely for the reasons of time or space. I used to have very little room to grow seedlings as growing on windowsills was not allowed (banned by the wife for making a mess and the cats used to eat the plants) so I would end up growing some vegetables from seedling such as pumpkins and then buying more common vegetables as seedlings.

Does the Vegetable Transplant Well?

Some vegetables do not mind transplanting, but others are going to object to being transplanted, and the shock, unless you are very careful, can damage the plant and stunt its growth. Typically root crops and those vegetables that have taproots (long, deep roots) do not transplant well and will need planting directly into the ground like seeds. Carrots are an example of this, which is why when you see carrot seedlings for sale, they are typically the globe carrot and not the long straight rooted variety we see in the stores.

Plants such as peas that grow quickly do not benefit from being started off from seed simply because they grow so fast and will soon catch up when planted direct.

Direct Seeded Vegetables

Some of the vegetables that are typically grown direct from seed are:

- Beans
- Beets
- Carrots
- Corn
- Cucumbers
- Garlic
- Lettuce
- Parsnips
- Peas
- Pumpkins
- Radishes
- Squash
- Turnips
- Watermelon

Transplant Seeds

Vegetables that transplant well and can be bought as seedlings include:

- Any herbs
- Broccoli
- Brussels Sprouts
- Cabbage
- Cauliflower

- Celery

- Chard

- Eggplant

- Kale

- Leeks

- Onions

- Peppers

- Tomatoes

You can also plant onions from sets, potatoes are grown from seed potatoes, and garlic is grown from cloves.

At the end of the day, it comes down to convenience and availability, but the above factors should be considered as they will influence your choice of what to plant. If you are short of space or a novice gardener, then I would recommend starting with seedlings as they are easier and eliminate germination, which can be a problem with some plants. Other plants like peas you can put in the ground and they will grow with no trouble and very little effort.

Chapter 7-   Sowing Seeds

Sowing Your Own Seeds

After you have selected the appropriate container and Soilless dirt (or developing medium), follow these steps to sow your seeds:

1. Fill the container with moistened growing medium to inside 1⁄2 inch of the surface of this container. Soilless mixes are dusty and hard to moist initially. Pour the mixture into a plastic bag, then add enough hot water to moisten the mixture but not twist it to some drippy sand pie. Mix the water and increasing medium with your palms or a solid wooden spoon, shutting off the start of the bag as far as possible to maintain the dust inside. Remove the dirt in the bag and set it in the container. Gently business down the medium using a flat piece of timber, including a ruler.

2. If you are planting seeds in a flat, follow along with Instructions to sow your seeds: Create shallow furrows (row like impressions) using a blunt rod or by pressing on the narrow edge of a ruler to the medium. Then sow the seeds based on those guidelines:

• Sow Small seeds, like carrot, at approximately five to eight seeds per inch, should you would like to transplant them to distinct containers shortly once they develop. Sow bigger seeds, like melons, at a few seeds per inch.

• Sow seeds sparingly, at three to four Seeds per inch, if you plan to lean and leave them at precisely the exact same container (instead of transplant into a bigger container). Either way -- transplanting the seeds into a fresh container or leaving them at precisely the exact same container -- works well; it is only a matter of what pots and space you've got. Transplanting into individual pots takes up more space but enables bigger plants such as berries more space for their roots to develop. Smaller crops, like lettuce, develop nicely when thinned and abandoned in their initial containers. It's possible to broadcast (randomly disperse) seeds instead of planting them into row like trenches, but row planting and thinning tend to be simpler.

2. If you are planting seeds into individual containers, here is the way you sow:

• Place 2 to four seeds in each container.

• Afterwards, thin the seedlings, leaving the strongest one.

3. After sowing the seeds at the correct thickness (see the appendix), cover them with nice grained soil or vermiculite. Label each container or row as most seedlings seem equal. You may buy labels from a nursery or via a mail-order catalog, or you may use old ones out of previously bought nursery transplants. Employing a waterproof pen, record the kind of vegetable, the number, and also the date in which the seed has been planted.

4. Water the seeds lightly with a mister or spray bottle. A more powerful flow of water may wash seeds to a single section of this container or transfer them too deeply into the ground.

5. Cover the container with a sheet of clean Plastic or a plastic bag to maintain the moisture. If needed, use modest bets to prop up the plastic so that it does not rest along with this ground.

6. Put the planted containers in a hot place. The cooler the temperature, the longer it requires your plants to emerge, so retain them hot and toasty! Some hot spots include the peak of your fridge or near your furnace. But be careful about how you water about electric appliances. You are also able to purchase heating mats or cables which keep the soil heat from below. Follow the package directions carefully. Never place containers in direct sunlight; the vinyl cover holds in the warmth, cooking your seeds into departure.

7. Verify the containers every day to ensure they are still moist but not wet that they mold. If you notice signs of mold, then loosen the cover and then allow air; the mold must vanish. You can also hook up a little fan to gently blow across the seedlings (minus the plastic cap), maintaining the dirt on the other side. But take care not to wash out the seedlings.

8. Whenever you find the green shoots Emerge, remove the plastic cap, and then move your seedlings to a place that offers lots of light along with the appropriate growing conditions for the vegetable. Until seedlings emerge in the soil, mild is unnecessary, with the exclusion of celery and lettuce seeds. Sow these seeds lightly pressing them in the ground or covering them quite lightly inch of nice soil, then place the containers at a bright place or place them beneath 40-watt incandescent lighting.

Supplying the proper Amount of Light and Heat

The Light your young seedlings get is among the most crucial aspects of great development. Putting the seedlings at a south-facing window is 1 alternative but not necessarily the top one. In a bright window, even plants get just a portion of the light they would acquire outdoors. Windowsill plants frequently become tall and spindly since they make too warm in connection to the light they get. Growing seedlings under fluorescent lighting is a fantastic means to maintain light-hungry plants contented. Regular cool-white, 40-watt fluorescent bulbs are all good for starting seedlings. When at all possible, set your lights up near a window so that the plants can get both artificial and natural lighting. The expensive grow lights which you can buy in a nursery or via a mail-order seed catalog create the wider spectrum lighting which crops need for flowering and fruiting (even though your seedlings are going to be from the garden until they are prepared to blossom). Regardless of what type of lighting that you have, use one pair of lights (typically two bulbs into a pair) for each 1-foot-width of the seedling-growing region and maintain the bulbs 2 to 4 inches in the tops of the seedlings constantly. Keep the lights on for no longer than 16 hours each day so that the plants can receive their normal rest interval. Inexpensive timers that turn the lights off and on automatically can be found at nurseries and hardware stores.

Watering your own Seedlings

Water brittle Seedlings with care, or you risk uprooting them. Mist them using a gentle spray Or water from the ground by placing your tank in a bowl of water only Long enough to the dirt surface to moist (maintaining them longer than this can harm the plants' roots). Following the surface is moist, remove the container in the water and let it drain. Maintain the soil surface gently moist but not soggy. Always water with lukewarm water, also attempt to do this early in the morning, if potential. This way, the foliage can dry quickly throughout the day to prevent disease issues. As your plants become more powerful, you can water using a sprinkling Can that's a raised, a nozzle which Breaks the water to several fine streams. Following the crops grow their initial set of leaves (the leaves to start as the seed germinates are known as seedling leaves, and the following settings are accurate leaves) and possess a larger root system, Allow the soil dry slightly between watering. Give the plants sufficient water. At one time that some of it runs out the drainage holes at the base of the Container, but not leave the container sitting. Overwatering Boosts damping-off disorder (see the sidebar "Coping with damping off") and reduces the quantity of air in the soil, causing a weaker root system.

Thinning and Transplanting

After seedlings develop their first pair of true leaves (or if onions or leeks, which send a single blade, are two inches tall), you want to narrow them or transfer them out of shallow flats to bigger quarters. Thinning is a significant measure, and timing is vital. Should you allow your seedlings to grow overly big in a small container, then their growth is stunted. And if you do not space out them at all, then you end up with weak plants. To thin plants which will keep on growing at exactly the exact same container, then snip out additional seedlings at the soil line using a pair of scissors. If you attempt to pull out these seedlings, you might disturb the roots of those plants which are staying. Also, make sure you snip any weak or plants that are stained.

Feeding your own Seedlings

Regular Fertilizing helps create strong, healthy plants. Some potting soils already have compost blended in, and in case you do not need to include more. For different forms, use a diluted water-soluble fertilizer to one-third strength (normally one tsp. of fertilizer for each gallon of water) to water your seedlings. Water together with the solution once per week.

Partner Sowing(Companion Planting)

A companion plant is one that offers some kind of advantage to other crops growing nearby. It is kind of like how a fantastic friend makes life simpler for you. Plants have great friends, also. These crops are ideal in repelling certain pests; plant them close to plants where pests of these kinds are a nuisance

✓ Anise Implanted among members of the cabbage family (broccoli, cabbage, cauliflower, kale, etc.) is believed to repel imported cabbage worms. It is a fantastic companion to tomatoes since these insects are feeding on this kind of plant

✓ Basil Is believed to repel aphids, spider mites and whiteflies;

✓ Catnip Is believed to have the ability to repel kinds of flea beetles, cucumber beetles, squash bugs and aphids.

✓ Garlic can eliminate soil pests.

✓ Leeks Are considered working against flies pestering carrots.

✓ Marigolds and mustard greens are designed to bug off aphids.

✓ Nasturtiums Are believed to repel Colorado potato beetles.

✓ Radishes can bug off cucumber pests

✓ Southernwood can eliminate the presence of fleas and moths.

✓ White clover can bug off flies pestering cabbages.

✓ Wormwood can repel beetles.

Chapter 8-   Watering

One of the most critical chores in any garden is providing the perfect balance of water to your plants. You can spend hours with a watering can visiting each plant every day.

Drip Irrigation and Soaker Hoses

The next logical step from dragging sprinklers all over your yard is the use of drip irrigation and/or soaker hoses. The nice part about these types of watering mechanisms is that they are less expensive to install, and yet they can be automated, which will save you so much time.

A secondary time-saving benefit is a fact that water is only delivered to the plant's roots, not the entire bed. That means that there will be less water available to weeds in the main body of the flowerbed. Win-win.

Soaker hoses are hoses made of a semi-permeable material that looks like rough rubber.   They allow water to leach out the walls of the hose whenever the water is turned on. Soaker hoses are woven throughout the flowerbed, maybe encircling a plant's root zone if it is especially thirsty, to deliver water to each plant.

In use, the water will slowly drip out, so you will have to allow several hours to overnight to deliver adequate moisture. You can check how much water is being soaked up by digging to find out how far down the soil is moist. Be sure that the water is flowing out of the pores of the entire length of the hose. If there is not adequate water filling the hose, the seeping water will stop short of the end of the hose resulting in dead plants.

Drip irrigation is made up of plastic hose-sized pipes that are laid throughout the flowerbed. To water each plant in the area, mini delivery hoses with water emitters are attached to the main hose. You control how much water is distributed to each plant through the number of emitters and the volume of water each emitter delivers.

The most common emitters deliver one-half gallon, one gallon or two gallons of water per hour. By mixing and matching, you can come up with just about any amount of water you will need. A little experimentation or internet research should point you to a good starting volume, and then you can take it from there.

You can run either type of system by hooking up a hose to the end and turning on the water. Once you have checked that everything is working as you would like, you can spread a pretty layer of mulch to hide the hoses. You should periodically check on the hoses and emitters to be sure they are still dripping correctly. If one gets plugged up, your first indication of the malfunction is likely to be a wilted or dead plant.

There are battery-powered regulators to automate the delivery of water to the hoses. They come in many varieties from very basic, one hose with one schedule, to multiple hoses and several schedules. These regulators really increase the "set and forget" capabilities for watering. For the winter, remove the batteries and store your regulators inside.

Fully Automated Watering

Automatic sprinklers are the most time-efficient form of watering. No hoses to lug around. No sprinklers to set. Best of all, it can be used to water both your flowerbeds and your lawn through a combination of pop-up sprinkler heads and drip irrigation.

You can create a schedule and watering zones that work for you and let the system carry it out. Automatic sprinklers are easiest to install before your lawn and flowerbeds are established. Retrofitting is more complicated but can certainly be done.

While being very time-efficient, automatic sprinklers also call for the greatest up-front investment. You must have electricity installed or available at the control box. Water must be piped and pumped to the access points you designate. The larger your garden, the more time-wise this option becomes.

You can set the zones on a schedule, sit back and enjoy your freedom. You will still need to periodically check the emitters if drip irrigation is a part of your system, but that are a quick process.

Self-Watering Pots

Self-watering flower pots are an amazing invention. They have a reservoir at the bottom of the pot that holds water. The base of the dirt in the pot is in contact with the water and will wick the water up to the rest of the soil as needed. Self-watering pots have come a long way throughout the years. There are even pots that have indicators to show you when the water reservoir needs refilling.

You could potentially reduce your watering commitments from twice daily in the heat of the summer to once a week or less. Multiply that by the number of pots you are working with, and you have the potential to save a significant amount of time throughout a whole season. You can escape for the weekend with a light heart, knowing that you will come back to well-watered, perky plants rather than pots full of wilted and brown leaves.

Planting in Containers in the Ground

I have a stock water tank in my back yard that I use as a pond. When I was planning things, I wanted to include plants that would logically be near ponds. Since the area was not soggy (It actually was on the dry side.) I planted my bog plants inside containers with few to no drainage holes. I sank the planters into the surrounding soil, so they looked like part of the grounds. The containers allowed the water-intensive plants to thrive in an otherwise inhospitable environment.

If the plants you want to use are true bog plants, you can get away with no drainage holes. Plants that are just moisture-loving will need a few small holes punched in the bottom of the pot. The object of the small holes is to provide an extremely slow drainage situation so that the soil will not "sour," i.e., have all the organic matters within the dirt rot away, eventually making the soil a stinky mess. Bog plants love sour soil, other plants don't.

Using slow draining pots buried in the soil allows you to expand the types of plants you can easily grow in your garden without expending extra time or effort. You can use this same idea with thick but pliable plastic or a piece of rubber pond liner that is pushed down into a hole and then filled with dirt. As long as the material used will not break down over time, you can use it.

Chapter 9-   Fighting Weed Wars

The key here is always to keep a covering over any bare spot of earth to avoid giving prime garden real estate to any weed seeds that seek to establish their weed kingdom and cause you grief for many years ahead. There are several ways to accomplish this task in the vegetable garden such as mulching, landscape fabric, green manures or cover crops and intensive vegetable planting to crowd out weeds. Use as many of these techniques as you can to protect your precious growing space from invasion.

The best thing I have learned about weeds is to stop them early, and keep the soil covered with mulch, landscape fabric, plant intensively or grow a cover crop to beat the weeds. The smart gardener walks through the garden every morning, looking for problem weeds and deals with them immediately. Young weed plants are easier to remove than older, more established plants. Weeds compete for water and nutrients needed by your vegetable plants, so you want to remove them as quickly as possible. When pulling weeds, it's important to remove them with the roots intact to prevent regrowth. Sometimes the root ball has to be dug out with a shovel or spading fork. Pulled weeds can be laid down on the soil to decompose, to add nutrition for other plants. Remove all the weeds before planting your seeds and transplants, so they have a big head start before weeds emerge. "If you control weeds for several weeks after transplanting or seeding, until the crop plants are well established, then weed every three to five weeks until harvest, your crop will produce without significant yield reductions," writes Miranda Smith. To suppress weeds, I use a combination of landscape fabric, mulch and planting my vegetable crops intensively or close together to cast shade over the weeds to stunt their growth.

Mulching. Every fall, we gather all the leaves, our five giant oak trees shower down upon us, along with those blowing into our yard, from the neighbor's tree across the street. He's got really good leaves. Lots of the land in the ditch, waiting to be rescued and put to good use in the garden. We bag up the leaves for future mulching, and most of them are taken to the compost bins to work their magic in creating rich, beautiful humus. We also use a wheat straw to mulch around the trellis area and to cover open ground. But there's one guy who takes mulching to another whole level. Soil always needs a covering, to preserve nutrients and suppress weeds. The method of preparing a garden bed is to begin by laying down a layer of 3-4 sheets of newspaper, on top of that add 3-4 inches of compost, then add 2-4 inches of wood chips to top it off. There is always a covering on the soil to prevent the growth of weeds. Any weeds that pop up are easily pulled and discarded.

Landscape Fabric or weed barrier is an excellent way to suppress weeds in the garden. In our garden, we buy 200-foot rolls of <u>Preen Contractor's Grade landscape fabric</u> from Sam's Club and pin it down along pathways and on open beds waiting for planting. The Preen costs about $30 a roll and is available starting in the spring. It saves us a lot of time clearing weeds. We tried some of the cheaper landscape fabric from home improvement stores, and it barely lasted one year before needing to be replaced. You want a heavy-duty landscape fabric or weed barrier that will last a few years. Preen comes with a 30-year guarantee. It is black to keep weed seeds from sprouting and is chemical-free. Preen helps the soil retain moisture. It also comes with some anchor pins so that you can tag it into the earth so that it won't fly away.

Cover crops or green manure is an advanced gardening technique that I am planning to introduce into my garden., told me how she sows wheat seed in her garden space in the winter to suppress weeds throughout her garden season. She practically has very little weeds in her vegetable garden. "Cover crops in the home vegetable garden need to grow quickly and compete with weeds, you can plant cover crops right after harvest. He advises gardeners to plant large-seeded cover crops like peas, hairy vetch, wheat, cereal rye and oats close together at the rate of 4 oz. Per 100 sq. Feet. Plant smaller seeds like buckwheat, mustard, and ryegrass by broadcasting and covering with a light layer soil at a rate of 1/6 lb. Per 100 sq. Foot. The cover crop should be mowed 3-6 weeks before vegetable planting and definitely before it goes to seed. Cover crops that are especially good at weed control are buckwheat and oats, apply at the rate of 4 oz. Per 100 sq. Feet. Crimson clover is an excellent weed suppressant, apply it at a rate of 1-2 oz. plus 2 oz. of oats or rye per 100 sq. feet. "Cover crop-weed competition is a race that you want the cover crop to win!"

How to Grow a Cover Crop

- Choose which season you will grow a cover crop, winter or spring
- Obtain fresh, viable seed.

- Prepare the soil for seeding by removing weeds.

- Plant at the right depth and rate.

- Feed and water your cover crop.

- Let your crop mature and cut before it goes to seed.

Intensive Planting. Another strategy for suppressing weeds is to plant your vegetable crops close together to shade out the weed plants, and then weed seeds can't grow. You want to plant your seeds or transplants tighter, bringing them an inch or two closer to one another, so there is no space for weeds. I like to use the spacing methods of <u>Square Foot Gardening</u>. The spacing seems just about right to me, so the weeds have to take a back seed to the main crop. I like to prepare my bed for planting, by smoothing out the top of the soil first, then taking the end of a rake or hoe and using the handle end to draw the one-foot squares in the bed. I get 48 squares in each raised bed. When the seedlings pop up, they crowd out the weed seeds.

Cornmeal can be spread on the soil as pre-emergent protection against weeds, and it's organic.

Hand-Pull Weeds

Yes, hand-pulling weeds aren't fun. But, if you hand pull a few weeds that pop up here and there, combined with other methods of weed control, such as mulching, then you will find it easy to manage the weeds in your garden. After all, if you use the mulching method, you shouldn't get many or any weeds, so you simply need to pluck a few from around your plants when they crop up.

When pulling weeds, you want a few tools. Firstly, you will want a good pair of gardening gloves to keep your hands safe. Using tools such as a hori-hori or a small trowel may also help with small weed work. However, this is backbreaking work if you are trying to pull up more than a few weeks.

Thankfully, there are other options that you can use on a larger project. There are a variety of stand-up weeding tools, one of the best is by Fiskars. This tool has a serrated stainless-steel claw in the bottom of the base attached to a long pole and a handle. You can easily place the tool on top of the weed, step on the base, twist the claw into the soil, and pull it back up. You can quickly pull many weeds in quick succession this way. Then, once you are done, simply pick up and throw out the weeds and cover the garden bed with mulch to prevent future weeds.

Flame Weeding

Flame weeding is a great option, not only for your garden but also if you want to keep your entire lawn organic! Rather than using herbicides to remove weeds between the cracks in the concrete, along the fence, or next to your driveway, you can use a propane torch or flame weeder. You can even adjust the flame so that it only affects a narrow range so that you can easily get weeds out of your vegetables and garden beds. But, you have to be careful when using them in the garden.

When using a flame weeder, it works best if you catch the weeds early before their roots have time to spread or they go to seed. There is no need to burn the weeds to a crisp, but you do want to burn them well enough to damage the cell structure. This will cause the weeds to die slowly. Flame weeding can kill the roots of some weeds, but not all. While they do a great job on annual weeds, it may not completely kill the roots of perennial weeds. These weeds may need a second burning if they crop back up. Thankfully, they do a good job of preventing perennial weeds from seeding and spreading.

Boil Weeds

One of the cheapest and easiest weeding methods is to boil water and then pour it over the plants. This method will kill any plant it is poured over, as they are unable to withstand the extreme heat. Not only that, but it will also kill soil life such as worms. You can easily use this method to kill weeds in a sidewalk, along your driveway, or next to a fence. Boiling water can also be used in the garden, but you must be careful. You don't want to accidentally boil your crops or kill the soil in your garden beds.

Use a kettle when boiling your weeds and ensure it is at a full rolling boil before taking it off the heat. The kettle you use should have a small spout so that you can easily control the amount of water you pour. Similarly, you should pour the water very slowly so that you can ensure you don't pour too much and kill soil life or other plants.

This method is extremely successful and non-toxic. While it will kill any plant, it is worth noting that perennial weeds, such as dandelions, which have a long taproot might come back if you don't kill the entire root system. With these weeds, you may want to dig a small hole with a trowel at the base of the plant. You can then pour the water to kill the entire taproot. Once done, immediately refill the hole with soil to prevent airborne weeds from sprouting.

Find the weed suppression strategies that work for you in your garden. Be adventurous. Avoid chemical weed killers, as many contain carcinogenic properties and can cause other illnesses. I like to think of gardeners as conductors of an orchestra, we bring in the different elements at different times, to address issues and we know what strategies will play to the strength of our garden, and to our abilities. So try some things that are new to you, I will try a cover crop this year, and I will probably wonder why it took me so long. In suppressing weeds, you will keep valuable nutrition reserved for your precious vegetable plants in the high performing garden.

Chapter 10- Maintaining Your Vegetable Garden

One thing that you may notice when you begin and maintain a garden is that you must perform ways on how to maintain the health of your plants.

Here are some general tips to remember when it comes to gardening.

Bugs and Pests

While your plants may be more protected from harmful insects, they're also missing out on the visitations of what are called beneficial bugs, those who help plants along in one way or another.

You need to be mindful of the damage that can still be done by harmful insects to your plants. Keep an eye on the leaves and stems from seeing if they seem to have holes in them; this is a sign that bugs are eating them. While a little bit of munching is not typically a problem, when leaves and stems start to wilt and fall off, this might be a sign of something that needs to be addressed.

One good way to address this problem is to introduce beneficial bugs to your plants. Beneficial bugs help your plants either by turning the soil or by feeding on those harmful insects. Beneficial bugs include ladybugs, butterflies, and earthworms.

By releasing these insects into your soil, they can help your plants be prepared for their environment, and of course, many will come with the plants when they get uprooted and put into a pot. If you have kids, you can even turn this into a fun activity for them - have them see if they can catch ladybugs in the backyard to bring into the outdoor or indoor garden, or you can have them dig up earthworms that you can put into larger pots of plants.

Introducing beneficial bugs is a common practice for those who are trying organic gardening as they can often forego the harsh pesticides and chemicals needed to address harmful insects.

About Pesticides

If you're tempted to use pesticides on your plants, you should be very careful about this practice. Because your plants are in a controlled and sealed environment, it means that those chemicals will be trapped inside the indoor garden and won't have a chance to dissipate into the atmosphere. Try using organic products as these are made from natural ingredients rather than synthetic chemicals and are less harmful to plants and the air inside your garden. Very often, just sponging off your plants can wash away harmful insects as well. And if you do decide to use pesticides on your outdoor or indoor garden plants, do so very sparingly. Remember that when you're in the garden, you'll be breathing those fumes as well as your plants!

Use Compost or Plant Food

This is probably some of the best advice you can remember about nurturing a garden. Why?

Soil outdoors gets replenished by the elements around it. When the soil is wet, nutrients travel under the surface of the ground, meaning that whatever you take out of the ground because of your plants will be replaced because of nutrients the soil draws from the surrounding ground.

This, of course, is just not possible with potted plants. All the nutrients that the soil will have are contained in that little pot. When your plants draw out those nutrients, the soil has no way of replenishing itself.

Using compost or plant food is vitally important for plants. Properly prepared Compost is full of nitrogen and carbon, two essential elements needed in the soil. Commercial plant food does the same thing.

You don't want to overfeed, of course, as this may interrupt the necessary balance of nutrients, but usually, you add something to the soil every two weeks or so. With compost, you simply spread it around the stem of your plant; it will get naturally absorbed into the soil every time you water your plants. Plant food brands will tell you how often they should be used.

Remember that plain water is not enough to keep your plants healthy and nourished. Water doesn't contain the vital nutrients that plants need and that are being stripped of the soil. You absolutely must use some type of food with your potted plants regularly.

Sunlight and Temperature

One common mistake that many outdoor or indoor garden owners make is to keep their structure or garden too warm and humid. They often believe that if a little bit of heat is good, then, even more, it will be better.

This just isn't the case. Unless you're growing all tropical flowers that need it to be very hot and humid all year long, you should have a moderate amount of sunlight and heat in your garden. Most common houseplants, flowering plants, and vegetable plants need comfortable temperatures and a reasonable degree of sunlight, not a very humid environment, and direct sunlight for many hours per day.

Don't be afraid of opening the vents of y indoor garden or of using that shade cloth during the warmest days when the sun is out for several hours. Your plants need that sunlight, but think of how you feel like a human sitting out in the hot sun for hours - after a while, it gets to be too hot, and the sun is damaging to your skin. Your plants are the same; they do need some sun and heat, but not an obscene amount of either!

There are a few factors that you may need to consider to succeed with outdoor or indoor garden gardening. Factors such as soil quality, watering, and maintenance can all influence your success. The following are what to pay attention to:

Soil Quality

Your choice of garden soil should contain potassium, phosphorus, and nitrogen, which are all necessary for growing healthy plants and foods. You can buy a potting mix at a nursery or local garden center. Most plants will flourish if the soil contains a PH ranging from 6.2-6.8. Use a soil test kit to determine the soil PH. The kit is also available at a nursery. Add compost to your soil annually to keep its growing quality.

Growing Crops

Fruits such as grapes and peaches will thrive in any garden environment. They do not need plenty of space. Vegetables such as eggplants and tomatoes will also flourish in both outdoor and indoor gardens. Before growing any plant in the structure, ensure to check on when to sow it and which variety will do best in an outdoor or indoor garden. You can obtain this information from a local garden center.

Chapter 11-   Nutrients and Fertilizing

Several signs will detect deficiency when the necessary nutrients are lacking in the plants.

A lot of these signs are quite easily detected, and they can also be similar to the other deficiency. Some of them, however, are quite distinct, but then since we are giving you quite something to worth your while, it is okay that you get the very symptoms of these, so you can easily.

Below is a list of the symptoms of deficiency for the elements that are needed by the hydroponic system for each of the elements; you should, however, note that these symptoms may be different for some crops, but this list should guide you to have an idea of what exactly the problem is.

Nitrogen;

plants that are deficient in this element are usually very short, the leaves are very pale looking and have some yellow spot colors on them. However, in the tomato crop, the leaves and the steps do not show yellow. Instead, they have a purple coloration underneath the leaves and on the stems.

Phosphorus;

Plants deficient in phosphorus have a dark green color, and also appear to be stunted; this symptom is first seen in the older leaves before the newer leaves. Also, there is a delay in the maturity of the plant. The weather can affect the uptake of nutrients by plants, and sometimes, the cold weather can be the reason why a plant show phosphorus deficiency and not necessarily because there is a lack.

Potassium:

For this element, a deficiency is suspected when the old leaves will become yellow, and then they are dark spots that are scattered around the leaves; the death of the plant soon follows this. When there is a severe deficiency, it will lead to stunted; all the leaves will be yellowed and curled. The lettuce crop will tend to appear bronze, and also this begins from the matured foliage.

Sulfur

This element is usually available, and the deficiency is not very common; there can be yellowing of leaves, and this can be seen in small and new plants grow.

Magnesium; this is quite common for the tomato crop when it does occur, there can be yellowing of leaves, and this happens between the vein and which remains green.

Calcium:

Deficiency in calcium affects the older leaves, and they become distorted; they are small in size because they have spotted and dead areas of the plant. This deficiency inhibits the development of bud, and the root tips will sometimes die back. When the tip burn occurs on the lettuce plant is a case of Calcium deficiency. When the root of the tomato crop blossoms, then it is a calcium deficiency, and this is seen as a deficiency in the fruit and not in the nutrient solution. And this is a transport problem within the plant; the plant has issues with transporting calcium from the nutrient media to its fruits. Several environmental factors can cause this problem.

Iron

This deficiency is quite distinct. It is seen as the yellowing of leaves while the veins remain green; this is first observed on the new leaves and growth. It differentiates it from magnesium deficiency, which begins its yellowing from older leaves. On other crops like tomatoes, iron deficiency can be because of the cold weather and not caused because of the actual lack of nutrient media.

Chlorine

This deficiency is seen as wilted leaves, and then the leaves become yellowed, they turn to bronze color and then become necrotic. The roots of plants that have chlorine deficiency will become stunted and have thick near their tips.

Manganese; there is a beginning yellowing at the intervener leaves of the older leaves, and this depends on the plant types. The leaves get dried and brown areas, and then they begin to drop.

Boron

When plants suffer from a deficiency in boron, the size of the plant begins to reduce; the plant, as it is growing, begins to die; there is a little bit of swelling that is noticed in the root system. The leaves are then thickened, they are yellow with some spots, and then they also appeared curled.

Zinc

A deficiency in zinc will result in stunted growth of the plants and a corresponding reduction in the internode and the size of the leave. The edges of the leave may become distorted and puckered; there can also be yellow spots between the veins.

Copper

it is quite hard to get a deficiency of this element. However, young leaves will have dark green colors, and they will become twisted, with dry and brown spots

Molybdenum; this affects the older leaves majorly because they will have yellowing between their veins; it then moves to the younger leaves; the edges of the leaves will then develop cupping of leaves.

Plants need nutrients to grow, flourish and battle off pests, diseases, and environmental anxieties. Giving them the nutrients they need is vital to fruitful organic gardening. Healthy soil that contains a lot of compost or organic matter goes a long path toward giving basic nutrients to plant growth. However, your plants may, in any case, need additional nutrients to grow to their maximum capacity. Right now, give you the lowdown on organic fertilizers — those got from a common plant, creature, and mineral sources — and how to utilize them.

Fertilizers 101

In contrast to soil revisions that improve the general soil environment, fertilizers are defined to give explicit plant nutrients in explicit amounts.

It's a legend that all plants need to be continued preparing all through the cultivating season. Plants growing in good soil — soil that possesses the best possible pH and is revised routinely with organic matter — may thrive fine and dandy without supplemental feeding. Trees, bushes, and perennials particularly adjust well to slow, steady growth. The fast growth animated by substantial treating, then again, can result in powerless, succulent plant tissue that is increasingly helpless to assault by insects and diseases and to harm from extreme climate.

Organic Versus Synthetic Fertilizers

Organic fertilizers, by and large, originate from minerals animals or plants. In general, organic fertilizers possess a variety of nutrients that also includes essential follow components; most are adding organic choices to soil and improve it. Paradoxically, fertilizers the explicit chemical recipes and frequently contain just three nutrients: potassium, phosphorous and nitrogen.

Organic fertilizers have different advantages compared to chemical fertilizers for the plants and soil.

✓ They release their nutrients all the more slowly in the soil when the plants need them, so they last longer.

✓ The nutrients are contained in complex atoms that won't leach away with the main rain.

✓ They are more averse to consume the youthful underlying foundations of small seeds. Chemical fertilizers are developed from salts (mineral) that can slaughter roots just as microbes whenever applied inappropriately.

✓ They improve soil health by supporting (or if nothing else not hurting) the soil microbes that assist make with soiling nutrients available to plants.

When all is said in done, organic fertilizers are the more gentle and kind approach to feed plants nutrients they must have.

Plant-Based Fertilizers

Plant-based Fertilizers have minimal to direct N-P-K esteems. However, their nutrients are easily and fast available to the soil for your plants to utilize. Most of the fertilizers give off an additional portion of the following nutrients and minerals.

✓ Alfalfa meal:

✓ Compost:

✓ Corn gluten meal:

✓ Cottonseed meal:

✓ Kelp/seaweed:

✓ Soybean meal:

✓ Humus:

Other plant-based organic fertilizers incorporate cocoa meal (might be toxic to pets), espresso beans, molasses, and nut meal.

Animal-based fertilizers

✓ Manures

✓ Bat/seabird guano

✓ Blood meal

✓ Bonemeal

✓ Fish products

Chapter 12-   Pest Control

There are plenty of common diseases and pests that affect herbs just as they do vegetable garden plants, so you want to keep an eye out for some of the following signs.

These pests will destroy just about any plant, so be sure to get rid of them as soon as you see them!

Aphids

These pests love the new leaves on herbs and can cause curling of the foliage if there are too many of them. The honeydew they secrete can promote sooty mold that will attract other pests, ants. They are commonly found amongst herbs that are too close together and rapidly growing herbs. Some neem oil and soaps will aid in getting rid of these.

Spider Mites

A serious condition for any container plant, spider mites like dry, hot conditions and are usually seen on the underside of herb leaves. Protecting the plants from this pest is as easy as using a strong stream of water that's aimed at the foliage and some regular irrigation.

Whiteflies

These will also appear on the underside of the leaves and can be gotten rid of using a strong stream of water.

Leafhoppers

They don't usually do a lot of damage, but you might see these guys eating your oregano, basil, and parsley. Just shoot them away by putting them in a different part of your garden or try spraying the leaves with a pepper spray.

Leaf Miners

These like to attack the succulent herb plants like basil, and they leave tunneling trails that go from the upper and lower leaf surfaces. Remove any affected leaves and take a look at your watering habits to see if the pots are too moist.

Parsley Worms

These are black swallowtail caterpillars that turn into beautiful butterflies. Therefore, most gardeners will plant plenty of the herbs they like to eat, such as parsley, fennel, and dill so that they don't have to worry about the little that the worms will eat.

Flea Beetles

Flea beetles are a rather harmless pest for most plants. They chew pinprick holes in the leaves but don't cause any lasting damage.

Weevils

These will feed on parsley roots, but, again, they don't cause a lot of damage and are not something to worry about.

Spittle Bugs

These insects don't cause a lot of damage to the plant, but they are disgusting, considering the leave a big glob of spit-like froth on the leaves and stems. They can easily be washed off with water.

Diseases

While most pests are not that too much of a concern for herb plants, the diseases can be troublesome. However, the solution is pretty simple. There are very few plants that thrive in waterlogged conditions, only mint and lemongrass, like wet soil, so you'll want to check your watering routine if you notice any form of disease on the plant.

Diseases on your herb plants will look like brown streaks on the stems, with the plant eventually dying. Rust plagues a lot of the mint family and looks like a rusty orange lesion son, the underside of the leaf.

The best defense against these diseases is proper growing conditions and removal of any infected leaves.

Pests Prevention and Treatment

Besides fruit and vegetables, plants also bring something else to your home—pests and disease. If you are new to gardening, the volume of bug and disease issues that you will be faced with can seem overwhelming. But don't worry. It isn't anything that you won't be able to handle with the right tools and the correct knowledge.

There are several ways to deal with these two unfortunate side effects of container gardening: prevention and treatment.

Prevention

It is always better to eliminate the possibility of problems before they have a chance to present themselves. While this is not always a 100-percent guarantee that you will be disease-free and bug-free, it will certainly go a long way in diminishing the number of problems that you have to deal with.

Rules of prevention:

1. Keep an eye out. Since your containers are isolated from other growth, you should be able to spot pests and disease as soon as they appear. Catching an issue early gives you a much better opportunity of keeping it contained to a small area. When you water your plants, give them an once-over. If you use a self-watering system, get in the habit of inspecting them periodically.

2. Maintain a healthy garden. Plants are much more susceptible to disease when they are sick themselves. Keeping your plants healthy is one of the best preventive measures that you can practice. Keeping your plants well-fed, with plenty of good, rich soil, and adequately watered will go far in helping fight off predators.

3. Start with healthy plants. Certain plants are more tolerant of some insects and diseases than others. Do some research to determine which varieties of plants are the hardiest. If you aren't sure when you are shopping for seedlings, ask a store associate. Sometimes, the information is given right on the plant's label.

4. Keep your tools clean. It's common for people to use their yard tools for more than maintaining their container garden. But moving them from fresh, potted soil to yard dirt can leave them open to picking up a wide range of unhealthy bacteria, fungus, and other nasty things. If you use your tools outside of your container garden, make sure to disinfect them thoroughly before using them again on your plants to avoid any kind of contamination.

Separate the good from the bad. If one plant comes down with a disease, chances are they all will unless you act quickly. Separate a plant at the first sign of trouble to avoid spreading it to others.

Treatment

Once bugs or disease hit, it's time to take action. The first thing people do is run to their closest garden center and load up on chemicals. But wait! You want to make sure that you are stopping the infestation while limiting the residual damage left behind to the plants and the environment. How do you do that? Research

To effectively deal with something, you have to know exactly what it is that you are being forced to deal with. Unless you are an expert in plant diseases and pests, you probably will not know what it is. Trying to describe a particular bug in detail or exactly what a specific kind of fungus or blight looks like a garden associate might not be accurate enough. You need proof.

If you can, capture one of the bugs or pull off an infected leaf and take it with you for identification. If you can't or don't want to, get your hands on a pest, write down exactly what it looks like including shape, size, color, any distinguishing marks, if it flies, crawls fast, has long antennae, etc. And if that seems like too much work, take a picture or video using your cell phone. Now, your sales associate will know exactly what to give you to fight it.

If you are given a pesticide, make sure of a few details before purchasing. First, is it specifically designed for just this one problem or a host of problems? Many pesticides are designed to kill everything that moves. While this might sound reasonable to a gardener who is closely guarding their container garden, it also means that even good insects are being eradicated. This is not advisable.

Some pesticides are only geared for specific pests. Going with this is always the best option.

Your second concern is its staying power. Does it quickly dissipate, or does it linger on the plant, and in the soil, for some time? If it hangs around, this means that good rain will wash it out into the yard and who knows where else. If the pests are on your plant, you do not want pesticides flooding your yard.

Believe it or not, some pests have their own traps named after them. Trapping them is a logical choice over using poison and is less messy.

Remember that anytime you use pesticides of any kind, you have to protect yourself. This means everything from wearing long sleeves and safety goggles to protective gloves—even when handling the containers.

Also, make sure not to try to use a chemical when there is even the slightest of wind since it will blow fumes or pesticides everywhere around you—including on you. And check the weather before you apply to ensure that a torrential downpour won't wash away your effort right after you apply it.

If you come across old pesticides, never pour it down the drain or even out into the woods. It will eventually creep its way back into your surrounding groundwater. Instead, call your county and ask for directions on how it should be disposed of. You can also call the manufacturer on the label, and they can advise you on how to dispose of it safely.

For those who wish to protect their plants while still keeping things healthy, there are natural alternatives. A little research will provide you with a list of natural, organic, and chemical-free alternatives that are proven to be effective while leaving the environment unscathed. Some of these might involve mixing certain commonly found household ingredients, but it's still better than putting out poison if it isn't necessary.

Chapter 13-   Cool and Warm Season Vegetables

Vegetable Types

The following are some general characteristics of each family.

Allium family - Alliums take a long time to mature. Onions can take 4-6 months; Garlic can take up to 9 months. Chives are fairly quick and great for containers. Garlic is planted from cloves, not seeds, pointy side up. Shallots, onions, leeks and chives can be grown from seed. Seeds do no remain viable as long as other families.

Beet family – Beets and Swiss chard have long taproots and are good for breaking up clay soil. Beets and chard do not like to be transplanted and are best sowed directly in the ground.

Dill family – Seeds of this family can take up to three weeks to germinate. For all you cooks out there, between the onions and garlic of the Allium family and the aromatics of the Dill family, you're halfway through French, Italian and other gourmet cuisines. Most sauces start with a mirepoix (or some derivative thereof), which is a combination of celery, onions and carrot. This family is also known for its flowers attracting beneficial insects, in particular, wasps. A carrot flower looks similar to Queens Anne Lace, also a member of this family.

Aster family - Chicory, endive, escarole and radicchio are all a little on the bitter side, but excellent when mixed with other lettuces. Lettuce is one of the easiest vegetables to grow, it just needs water. It will bolt in hot summer months, so if growing, then a little late afternoon shade or misting would be helpful.

Bolting means the plants send up a central stalk to flower and seed. Once lettuce bolts, it is over. It becomes very bitter at that point.

Brassica family - The Brassica family is the largest family of edibles. On the whole, they are very tolerant of cool weather. Kale and Brussels sprouts, in particular, can take a little frost. Kale is one of the most nutritious vegetables you can eat. They contain a lot of phytonutrients. Phytonutrients are certain organic components of plants that are thought to promote human health.

Melon family - Up till this point, we're eating not only cool-weather crops but also mostly vegetation (leaves). Yes, carrots and radishes are roots, broccoli and artichokes are immature flowers, but mostly we are eating vegetation.

However, now with the warmer weather and more importantly, the longer periods of daylight, we are eating fruits. It takes a lot of plant energy to make flowers and fruits.

In the summer months, when the sun rises at 6:00AM and sets at 8:00PM, we have 14 hours of sunlight. Compare that with December when the sun rises at 7:00AM and sets at 5:00PM. That's only 10 hours of sunlight. Those extra 4 hours of sunlight (40%) is what enables the plant, through photosynthesis, to provide the energy to create fruits.

Botanically speaking, cucumbers, melons, pumpkins, etc. are fruits. They are derived from a flowering plant and are how these plants disseminate their seeds. Most edible fruits were evolved by the plants to exploit animals (and man to a certain extent) as a means for seed dispersal. Animals eat the fruit and pass the seeds along into their stool.

Melons, Pumpkins, Winter Squash and Watermelons all take up a lot of room. They grow on vines that can easily reach 8-10ft in length. Chayote vines can reach 25 ft. Think of all those leaves as mini solar panels collecting sunlight for photosynthesis.

Legume family - Bean and pea plants fix nitrogen in the soil through their root system. When planning your garden, it's a good idea to follow a legume with a big nitrogen feeder like corn or broccoli or any in the melon/pumpkin family to take advantage of the excess nitrogen in the soil.

Mint family -This is our herb family. All are perennials, but basil, all can take cool weather well except for basil (there's always one in every family). Because they are all perennials, you may want to group them all together and reserve one section just for herbs. That's also part of planning.

Mint and oregano reproduce by sending out runners. If not kept in check, it can become invasive like a weed. Many like to grow it in a container for that reason.

Grass family - Corn is one of the most popular vegetables for the home gardener. Though corn requires plenty of space in the vegetable garden, it is hard to beat its taste and tenderness, especially when freshly picked. Corn can grow to a height of 7-8 ft. And should be planted at the northern end of your garden so as not to shade the other plants.

Nightshade family - Edible members of the nightshade family include eggplants, potatoes, and peppers. The spice, paprika, is made from dried red peppers. Tobacco is also a member of the nightshade family; in fact, the edible members all contain trace amounts of nicotine.

Leaves and stems from the nightshade family should not be eaten, and care should be taken that pets do not eat them as well. The nightshade family is notorious for its poisonous plants, including belladonna and jimson weed.

Misc. – Other vegetable families we need to be aware of are:

Asparagaceae, edible member, Asparagus and Convolvulaceae, aka the Morning Glory Family, edible member, Sweet Potato.

The majority of edible plants in a backyard garden are members from one of ten Vegetable Families. Families are the way vegetables are classified in the plant world. Each family is unique in the way that they flower and fruit (carry their seed).

It is good practice to plant all varieties of one family together in one bed. The reason is two-fold:

1. What's good for the goose is good for the gander, or in other words, what's good for the broccoli is also good for the cabbage. Plants varieties of one family usually share the same sun requirements, water requirements, and nutrient requirements.

2. Planting your family varieties together facilitates crop rotation. We rotate crops to not plant the same plant in the same place year after year. The reason is so soil born insects, and pathogens do not congregate and cause harm to the plant. By rotating the plants, you are effectively taking away the pests' food source.

The list below contains the names of the ten families along with the more popular varieties. Cool Weather Families are listed first. The remainder is Warm Weather Families. (Italics) are contrary to the rule, which means they are grown in the alternate season.

Cool Weather Families

1.Onion or Allium Family

Edible Members: onions, chives, shallots scallions, leeks garlic,

2, Amaranth or Beet family

Edible Members: epazote, spinach, quinoa, amaranth, chard beet

3.Dill or Carrot Family

Edible Members: cumin, parsley angelica, parsnip, caraway fennel, cilantro, anise, dill, celery, carrot, chervil, celeriac,

4.Aster family

Edible Members: dandelions radicchio, artichokes, escarole cardoons, chicory, endive, , lettuce,

5Mustard or Brassica Family

Edible Members: kohlrabi, turnip, rutabaga broccoli, rapini Brussels sprouts, cabbage, radish cauliflower, mustard collard, kale

6. Legume family

Edible Members: peas, (peanuts), (soybeans), lentils (beans), fava beans

7. Mint family

Edible Members: (shiso), thyme (basil) rosemary mint, marjoram, sage, oregano,

Warm Weather Families

1. Squash family

Edible Members: pumpkin cucumber, watermelon chayote, melon, squash,

2.Grass family

Edible Members: bamboo sugarcane barley, corn, rice, rye, wheat

3. Nightshade family

Edible Members: tomato eggplant, (potato), peppers

Chapter 14-   Growing Herbs

Chives

Chives are delicious, thin, green leaves that exude the taste of garlic. This herb is one of the most preferred as it will grow in any weather. You can chop it up and add it to your soups or use them to garnish your salads and other dishes.

Here is how you can sow, grow and harvest your chives.

- Plant your chives in early spring as they prefer the cold climate.

- The soil has to be well moisturized, rich in nutrients and needs to be quite porous.

- Before you plant the plants in the soil, you can start them indoors in a little nursery, and you can do this eight weeks in advance.

- If you did not do this or did not have time for it, then plant the seeds in the soil as soon as it is workable.

- Ant your seeds at a distance of 6 inches and place them at least ½ inch deep.

- Remember that the chive plant is a heavy drinker, and you need to water it heavily and regularly to have a heavy yield.

- You can make use of a good amount of mulch to allow it to stay moisturized.

- The plant will thrive if ignored, and all you have to do is water it a bit daily.

- Fertilize it regularly.

- Remember that the flowers are extremely pretty but need to be regularly removed as the seeds are extremely potent, and your entire garden might be covered in chives if you don't trim it.

- Chives can be harvested in 2 months after seeding, and they need to be stored in a cool place to last longer.

Mint

Mint leaves are probably the oldest known herbs on earth. The leaves look great, and the tiny flowers that the plant produces add a dash of color to the garden. Simply chop the leaves roughly and add to your salad, and you can also use it to make a mint chutney that will go with most of your dishes. Some people also use mint leaves to dry them up and place them in small bowls all over the house to help propagate a calming and rejuvenating smell.

Here is how you can sow, grow and harvest your mint.

- You can beg, borrow or steal for a few mint leaves, and that is all that you will need to grow your plants.

- You can buy yourself a fresh bunch from the supermarket or your grocery store and pick out the freshest ones with the thickest stems.

- Insert them at a distance of 3 inches and water them.

- You can also start them in a bowl of water just like the lemongrass, and once the stalks develop roots, you can transplant them.

- The plants love full sun and need to be watered regularly and heavily.

- Make use of a thick layer of mulch on top to help seal the moisture.

Your mint plant will multiply like crazy, and so you must keep an eye on it. Many people avoid planting it next to their favorite plants, as mint will start to take over in no time at all.

Mint takes no more than a month to grow new stems and fresh leaves and make sure you pinch the base of the leaves to harvest them.

Rosemary

Rosemary has a very sweet smell and a sweeter flavor. You can use it in Italian cuisine as well as flavor soups, salads, etc.

Here is how you can sow, grow and harvest your rosemary.

- It is easy to grow rosemary from the seeds.

- Buy yourself some good quality seeds from the nursery and give them a head start in an indoor nursery.

- Transplant them after the threat of frost has passed.

- Plant them at a distance of at least 8 inches wide and remove weak plants after a month as the healthy ones can grow to a height of 4 feet and also grow 4 feet wide. So you can have one plant at every 24 inches gap.

- You can plant your rosemary close or next to cabbage, beans, sage or carrot plants as the herb loves these plants and will thrive in their company.

- The plants love full sun. Also, water it every day, especially during the growing season, to have good growth.

- It is a good idea to plant this herb in containers as you will be able to shift it into the house during winters.

- Rosemary is best consumed as fresh as drying. It might cause a loss of flavor.

Sage

The sage herb is quite a flavorful herb and can have soft green, white or purple leaves. The herb is used in Italian and Spanish cuisines and mostly used for stuffing. Sage leaves can be chopped into small pieces and added to dishes or sprinkled over your salads.

Here is how you can sow, grow and harvest your sage.

- It is easy to grow sage from seeds, but the best way is to make use of cuttings from an established plant.

- You can plant the plants in well-draining soil and plant it before the last spring frost.

- Make sure that the soil temperature remains between 60 and 70 degrees Fahrenheit.

- You can plant them at 24 inches apart and insert them 2 inches deep into the soil.

- Planting them close to cabbages and cucumbers will help your sage plants thrive.

- Spring is the best time not just to harvest your sage plants, but also prune and trim them.

- You can remove the woody stems if they are barging into other plants.

- Although these are perennials, you should root them out every 5 years and have new ones grow in their place.

- Once you harvest them, you can dry them and store them in a cool and dry place, but they will only taste best when fresh.

Thyme

The thyme plant is extremely beautiful with long branches, short leaves and colorful purple and pink flowers. But given how most people only look at their dried form, the plant does not get appreciated for its natural beauty. It is extensively used in European cuisine. You can chop it roughly and add it to your tomato sauce, or you can also add it to your curries.

Here is how you can sow, grow and harvest your thyme.

- You will find it tough to grow the plant from seeds, and you should get quality cuttings from an established plant.

- To have the best results, you can plant the cuttings 6 weeks before the last spring frost.

- Make sure the temperature of the soil remains above 60 degrees Fahrenheit.

- Thyme does not need too much water, and if you water it in excess, then you might end up using it rot. Water it for no more than thrice week and don't over care for it.

- It will require full sun, so place it in a bright spot.

- You can fertilize the soil regularly.

- Planting it in a container will allow you to shift it inside

- Although you can store it by freezing or drying, you can also use them fresh.

Chapter 15-   Growing Vegetables (A-C)

Artichokes

These perennials are grown for their flower buds – usually unopened ones with a pine cone-like shape. Although most parts are actually edible, it's the flowers that you'd usually find in the grocery aisle.

Description

These plants can grow up to 6 feet with leaves that are long, arched, and prickly. They can spread up to 5 feet wide, making it important to give them sufficient space to grow. Artichoke is actually a general term, they can also be classified as their different species names: globe artichoke, green artichoke, and French artichoke. Growing each one is no different from growing the others.

Hardiness – Ideal Environment

Artichokes prefer the sun – which is why it's important to grow them in areas where they get the most sunlight. They fall within the USDA Hardiness Zones 7 to 11, which mean that your weather should be primarily sunny with winters that reach around 50 to 60 degrees Fahrenheit. Summers should be between 70 to 80 degrees for these plants to thrive.

Planting Artichokes

There are three ways to start planting artichokes:

Seeds– You'll find artichoke seeds in most gardening stores. Like most seeds, they are best started in a controlled container, using fluorescent lights to affect the seed's environment better. It's best to find a starting tray with at least 4 inches of soil – no need to make it big as you'll be transplanting this after 8 to 10 weeks.

Shoots/Roots– You can also try growing artichoke from shoots or roots. Dormant roots are often sold through stores. Make sure to choose a rooted shoot from a young plant – possibly no more than 10 inches in height. With rooted shoots, you can plant them directly in your ideal space.

For best results, every artichoke plant should be spaced at least 4 feet apart to offer room for growth.

Caring for Artichokes

Soil– Artichokes require lots of nutrients, especially the seeds. This is why it's crucial to prepare your soil beforehand to ensure that they'll get the most out of it. Fortunately, you don't need anything complicated. An organic fertilizer such as rabbit droppings, chicken droppings, and fish emulsion are common choices. Add 1 cup of organic fertilizer for every plant. Note that healthy soil is almost always loose and well-tilled. This ensures that although it can soak up moisture, the water doesn't stand still in the soil, which can cause rotting.

Watering – The soil must be kept moist at all times, especially during the dry weather. A good way of preserving moisture to prevent large water expenses is through mulching.

Weather Protection – Artichokes do well with full or partial sun exposure. The cold weather is their biggest enemy, which is why, in the United States, they thrive best in sunny areas such as California. Make sure to protect your artichokes during the cold season.

Pests – Slugs and aphids are typically the biggest enemies of the artichoke plant.

When and How to Harvest

When the artichoke reaches the size of a golf ball, it's time to harvest. You'll find that one primary bud matures faster – don't wait for it to flower! Quickly cut the bud from the stalk with one quick slice just beneath the bud while waiting for others to reach their harvesting size. The first bud should appear within two years, but the plant itself will be fully mature in just 100 days. Note that if you allow the plant to flower, it might not produce as heavily for the next year, so make sure that each bud is harvested as it comes.

Broccoli

Broccoli is a hungry and thirsty plant; it needs fertile, friable soil with good moisture-holding capacity. It also needs a lot of nitrogen, so work in 3 or more inches (8-plus cm) of compost or well-aged manure and some leaf mold. (Or add some chopped leaves to the soil the previous fall.) If you don't add greensand and rock phosphate to your compost, add both to your soil for this and other cabbage-family crops. Broccoli prefers full sun and a pH of 6.5 to 7.5.

Sowing

For an early summer harvest, sow broccoli seeds indoors about four to six weeks before the last spring frost. Seeds will germinate in about six days at 75°F (24°C). Once plants show true leaves, fertilize with an organic fertilizer such as fish emulsion at half strength. For a second, or fall, crop, direct-seed in late spring in cool regions and summer in warm areas. Don't start broccoli too early or too late. If you plant too early, you'll end up with large, root-bound transplants that may produce tiny broccoli heads, or "but-tons." Long exposure to cold weather can also produce buttoning. On the other hand, if your summers are very warm, don't plant broccoli too late; in hot weather, it may bolt before the heads are fully formed.

Growing

Broccoli transplants well, but are careful not to disturb the roots. Plant in a staggered pattern 16 inches (40 cm) apart, with 12 inches (30 cm) between rows. Three rows can fit in a 36-inch-wide (0.9 m) bed.

Fertilizing

If you've added enough organic matter and fertilizer to the soil, you probably won't need to fertilize more during the year unless you see signs of deficiency (slow growth, pale green or yellowish leaves, purplish leaf stems).

Harvest

The part of the broccoli plant we gardeners want is actually a large cluster of flower buds that would if we permitted it, become myriad small, yellow blooms. Harvest when the bud cluster, or head, is dark green and fully formed, with tight buds and no hint of yellow. Cut the head with a sharp knife. More, smaller heads will soon form as side shoots, a process that can continue until hard frost finally kills the plant. The more you harvest, the more you get. The plant will stop sending out new shoots if some of them finally get to the flowering stage. Some varieties are better than others at this game; I like to pick the ones that produce lots of shoots for a long time.

Carrots

Carrots are not difficult to grow, although they are known to take their sweet time to sprout.

However, do not give up slowpokes in the garden, they are worth it. Orange is the word of the day when it comes to carrots, but I'm willing to change everything. When you grow your own, 1,000 delightful (and beautiful) doors open. Surprisingly, carrots are available in red, white and purple, as well as combinations of orange and red.

Planting Carrots

Before planting carrot seeds, mix a generous amount of compost in the soil. They prefer loose, clayey sand to give their roots the leeway they need.

Carrots don't like to have disturbed roots, so they are generally planted directly in the garden bed. Sprinkle the tiny pin seeds on the loose soil 2 weeks before the last frost date.

The trick with carrot seeds is not to let the soil dry before they germinate, so keep the seedbed moist at all times.

These seeds are the smallest little things, and some gardeners add them to the sand in the shakers and then spread them on the garden bed. Usually, I explain to them and dilute them later.

Plant them from 1⁄4 "to 1⁄2" deep and spaced about 2 "apart in rows from 6" to 8 "apart and cover lightly with the soil. It takes 10 to 21 days to germinate eternity concerning other seeds.

If you want to speed things up a little, soak them in water for 24 hours the day before planting them. If you are stuck with a heavy soul (clay) for the season, plant the ball-shaped carrots instead of the typical, tapered and long-rooted types.

Tending Carrots

You will have to lose the seedlings when they are about 2 "tall. The first time you do it, it will seem brutal. But if you want to give them room to grow properly, you will show them a hard love.

Seedlings that is closer than 2 "together are gently pulled out or cut with a pair of small scissors on the soil line. In my opinion, using scissors is better because it ensures that the other roots of the seedling are not disturbed.

Harvesting Carrot

Carrots can be harvested when they are young enough (and more tender) or when they are fully ripe, i.e., when they are at the sweetest point. Check the days when the individual varieties are harvested, but most carrots are ripe 2 to 3 months after sowing their seeds.

If the soil is loose and crumbly, it will slide out with a slight tug at the base of their green buds. But if the soil is dry or hard, use a garden fork to loosen it; you don't want the suggestions to break during the collection. Just slide the fork deep under the carrot roots and waist gently. Like most vegetables, the flavor is better when they go straight from the garden to the table.

Chapter 16-   Growing Vegetables (E-K)

Eggplants or Aubergines

Many of us are familiar with eggplants that look like big purple tears. However, once you start examining the varieties, you will find that they can be as small as eggs or fingers. They can be green, lavender, pink, white or striped. Eggplants need a warm climate.

Planting Eggplants

Start the eggplant seeds at home 4-6 weeks before the last frost. Some people prefer to start them directly on the garden bed because they may not transplant well. Having said that, I always started them early because I needed the jump on the days when they need to mature and have done well.

Keep in mind that these seeds need 75 ° F soil to germinate, so this would be the time to indulge in the luxury of a thermal mat.

Plant the seeds 1⁄4 "deep and 1" apart. Once they are out in their bed, they should be planted about 2 feet apart. With eggplants, it's always about the heat. So, before you take them out, make sure that the night temperatures stay consistently above 55 ° F.

Tending Eggplant

Keep the aubergines watered evenly; never let the soil dry out. You can give them a balanced fertilizer when they start to bloom; then, every two weeks, give them the fish emulsion.

Harvesting Eggplant

Collect eggplants when they are fully colored (whatever the color for the variety) and while they are still shiny. If they become boring, you have waited too long. Use the pruners and cut them about 1 "above the eggplant. Like many other vegetables, the more you harvest, the more plants they will produce.

Garlic

Garlic forms a bulb made up of numerous individual cloves. There are several different cultivars available worldwide, but they are very similar, the main differences being taste and pungency. The skins are usually white but can be tinged to a lesser or greater extent with purple. The only other differences are the size and number of cloves, hardiness and storage qualities.

Planting

Use a dibber to make holes in the ground for each clove, at 10-15cm/ 4-6in intervals. A line of the string will help you to keep the row straight. Plant the cloves just below the surface, firming them in so that they are covered to their own height with soil.

Cultivation

A sunny open position is required, and, as with other members of the onion family, light soil is preferred. Use soil that has been manured for a previous crop or, if you are planting in spring, dig in the manure in the preceding autumn

Harvesting

Lift the bulbs when the leaves have turned yellow. Spread them out in a sunny place, preferably undercover — on greenhouse staging is ideal. When they have dried out thoroughly, remove any dirt and any long roots. If you are plaiting them or tying them in bunches, the leaves will need to be left on.

Pests and diseases

Garlic is relatively pest-free. It can, however, suffer from various fungal or viral diseases.

Horseradish

Some people claim to grow horseradish, but this vegetable is so easy it really grows itself. Rather than growing from seeds, this perennial develops from pieces of roots called root cuttings. You just plant the cuttings and stand back. The first season, let the plants grow and develop strong roots.

PLANTING AND GROWING

In spring, add a bit of compost or well-rotted manure to the spot where you plan to grow horseradish. Loosen the soil with a fork to a depth of about a foot (30 cm) as you mix in the compost or manure. After raking the bed smooth, dig a furrow about 6 inches (15 cm) deep. Set horseradish root cuttings along the side of the trench so that buds are toward the soil surface. Cover roots with about 2 inches (5 cm) of soil and water well. The shoots should appear in about a week or two.

HARVEST

After the first hard frost, loosen the soil around the plants with a garden fork. Lift the plants gently from the soil with the fork, trim off the tops, and brush the roots with a clean scrub brush to remove most of the soil. Remove some of the side shoots to replant.

Kale

Sea kale is a very hardy perennial vegetable grown for its uniquely flavored stems, which are eaten raw. The young flower heads and very young leaves can also be eaten raw, and the leaf midribs cooked. An established plant can be 3ft (90cm) in diameter with stems up to 2ft (60cm) tall. Each plant yields 8–10 stems. Sea kale is usually propagated from root cuttings or "thongs."

Site and soil

Sea kale needs an open, sunny site and a deep, rich, sandy soil, with a pH of 7 lighten heavy soils by adding grit or sand. It is closely related to brassicas, so occasionally suffers from club root

Sowing and planting

Plant thongs in early spring. Raising plants from seed is an alternative if you cannot obtain thongs. Scrape the corky coverings from the seeds with your nails; if not removed, these will inhibit germination. Sow thinly in seed trays from late winter at 45–50°F (7–10°C) and prick out seedlings into 4in (10cm) pots Plant out the seedlings in early summer when they are 3–4in (8–10cm) tall. Alternatively, sow thinly in drills in spring, and thin out the seedlings later.

Routine care

Remove any flowering shoots to concentrate energy into the stems. In spring, mulch with well-rotted manure, or top-dress with low-nitrogen fertilizer or liquid feed. When the plants die back in fall, follow the procedure for forcing outdoors to blanch the stems.

Harvesting

Cut the forced stems when they are ready). Stop cutting in late spring to allow the plant to regenerate

Chapter 17-   Growing Vegetables (L-P)

Lettuce

Planting lettuce

Lettuce is a cold worshiper, so plan on planting seeds in early spring or late summer / early fall. By the way, if you have a frame house or a cold frame, lettuce can be harvested all winter in most areas.

I spread the small seeds on the soil (or a mix out of the soil if they are at home), and I cover them lightly with the earth. The seedbeds are kept uniformly moist, when the seedlings are about 1 "tall, I lose weight from 6" to 8 ".

Begin your first spring lettuce crop indoors about 4 weeks before the last frost, then take it to the yard after the last frost date has passed. The next sowing should be done directly on the garden bed in late spring. In the autumn or early winter, plant more in a cold environment; This will allow you to take advantage of the sun, but will prevent freezing temperatures from killing the tender leaves.

Caring for Lettuce

The idea is to keep the soil around the lettuce as fresh as possible while preventing the sun from hitting the lettuce. Climbing vegetable crops like beans or tomatoes can help.

Plant your lettuce on the shady side of the taller types.

Harvesting Lettuce

Lettuce is in a hurry to come and pick. Take advantage of this by staggering your crop for a consistent salad crop. I know a gardener who plants lettuce in some large pots in his yard. Plant a few pots, wait a week and then plant another pair of pots.

For young tender vegetables, you can start picking lettuce leaves when they are only a few centimeters high.

Onions

Onions grown for their bulbs can be temperamental, as they like cool temperatures when they first start growing and then need the heat to produce their bulbs. Green onions are much easier to grow and are great for container gardens. Both varieties require rich, well-drained soil that is free of debris.

QUICK TIPS FOR GROWING ONIONS

Location: Sunny, moist but well-drained area

Best Soil: Rich, well-drained, light soil free of debris, pH 5.6–6.5

When to Plant: Transplants are usually available in early spring; onions can also be started from seed indoors and then transplanted outdoors.

Weeding: Need to be kept well weeded

Watering: In the early stages of growth, onions need lots of water, so keep the soil moist. Stop watering once the leaves start to turn brown.

Care Onions like rich soil, so when preparing the garden bed, make sure you add in several inches of compost or aged manure.

Fertilizing: Side dress with compost (place around the base of the plant) when the bulb first starts to swell, and again when the leaves are about 1 foot tall.

Pests and Diseases: Very few pests or diseases are found in onions, and the best way to prevent them is to use crop rotation.

Harvesting: When growing sets for green onions, harvest once the greens are about 12 inches tall. For the bulb, pull it up once the leaves have turned brown and died back.

Potatoes

Plant your potatoes as early as you can get into your garden. They are grown from cuttings from stems, which are known as seed eyes or pieces; the eye is where the new sprout will grow.

If you live in a mild climate, potatoes are hardy enough that they can remain in the garden all winter, if well mulched, and can be harvested as you need them. They need a fair amount of space as the roots can grow quite large.

QUICK TIPS FOR GROWING POTATOES

Location: Areas with ample sunlight. Well-drained but moist area. Potatoes thrive in cool weather.

Best Soil: Fertile, slightly acidic, sandy loam soil, pH 4.8–6.0

When to Plant: Seed them as soon as you can work for your garden bed in the spring.

Watering: Water regularly from the time the vine first emerges above ground until the plant flowers. After flowering, the plant needs less water with normal rainfall, usually being sufficient if the plants are mulched.

Care: Keep mounding (hilling) soil up around the vine as it grows; this helps to keep the potatoes covered.

Fertilizing: Fertilize with compost tea once the flowers start to emerge.

Harvesting: New or small potatoes can be harvested once the plant has flowered by digging around under the vine and pulling out a few tubers. When the vine turns brown and dies back, the tubers are fully mature. Then the whole plant can be pulled; use a garden fork to dig up the larger tubers gently.

Chapter 18-   Growing Vegetables (R-T)

Rhubarb

These plants can grow up to 3 feet in height and width, depending on the exact variety. For this reason, it's best to give rhubarb around 1 to 2 feet of spacing during planting, with the rows preferably around 36 inches apart. Typically classified as a perennial, your well-cared-for rhubarb plant will continue to be productive for more than five years.

Hardiness – Ideal Environment

The beauty of this plant is that it is capable of surviving both hot and cold weather. Your rhubarb must be planted somewhere where it gets full sun for at least four hours.

Planting Rhubarb

One important thing to keep in mind with this plant is that it doesn't do well when transplanted. Hence, you'll have to pick a spot with the idea of permanence. The best time to grow rhubarb would be in autumn or spring.

Caring for Rhubarb

Rhubarb thrives in moist but well-draining soil. Note that it's also possible to grow rhubarb in pots, but make sure that you till the soil properly to prevent rotting of the roots.

Watering – This plant can be pretty hardy, but watering it well during the summer makes it more productive than ever. Make sure that the roots are loose and drain well; otherwise, you might have to worry about bud rotting.

Pests – Since the leaves are poisonous, there are very few pests the rhubarb plant has to deal with.

When and How to Harvest

Rhubarb should not be harvested after the first year so that the plant can really get established. You can start harvesting in the second year, waiting for the stalks to become thick and reddish before cutting them off..

Summer Squash (Cucurbita pepo and maxima)

Many varieties of summer squash are types of shrubs (including many varieties of squash), which are perfect for vertical container gardens. But if you are planting a trellis or other structure, look for types of climbing plants.

Planting Summer Squash

Pumpkin seeds can be started indoors 3-4 weeks before the last frost date, or they can be planted directly in bed. Pumpkin is not thrilled that its roots are manipulated, but if you handle indoor crops carefully, they will be fine. The soil should be 70 ° F if you plant them directly in your bed.

Harvesting Summer Squash

Zucchini should be harvested when the fruits are 4-6 inches long. Patty pan squash and scallops are harvested even when they are small, around 2 "to 3" around and no larger than 4 ". Collect the bull neck when they reach about 3" to 4 "and the straight neck when they reach 4" at 5."

Tomatoes

Tomatoes offer more of a harvest per cubic inch of space than any other vegetable plant. There are dozens of varieties available so you can choose the variety you like.

QUICK TIPS FOR GROWING TOMATOES

Location: Sunny and warm area

Best Soil: Fertile, well-drained, pH 5.5–6.8

When to Plant: Set out transplants once the weather is warm, usually late spring or early summer.

Companion Plants: For a positive effect, a plant with asparagus, basil, cabbage, carrot, onion, parsley, peas, and sage. Potatoes and fennel can have a negative effect, so avoid planting close to tomatoes.

Weeding: Keep well weeded, especially when the plant is young.

Watering: Water deeply once a week.

Fertilizing: Fertilize with fish fertilizer or compost tea two weeks before and again two weeks after the first picking. If grown in pots or hanging baskets, fertilize every ten days.

Harvesting: Harvest all your tomatoes, even the green ones, before the first frost. Green tomatoes will ripen if left in a warm area.

Storage: Ripe tomatoes will not store for more than a few days. Green tomatoes will ripen indoors if left in a warm spot.

Chapter 19- Ways To Extend Your Growing Season

The main objective of planting vegetables is to garner as much yield as you can throughout the year while also maintaining soil health and sustainability.

Overwintering

There are three things that you can do to provide a healthy winter season for your garden: one, continue to grow appropriate crops; two, plant a cover crop that will both re-energize your soil with nutrients and provide warming ground cover; three, mulch the garden well to prevent degradation of topsoil. Or, of course, you can employ a mix of all three.

You can also overwinter certain root vegetable crops such as potatoes, parsnips, and carrots. If you live in regions where winters don't stay too cold for too long—that is, the ground does not stay in a state of hard freeze for an extended time—you can also overwinter several varieties of greens such as collards, kale, and heartier varieties of spinach and arugula. Keep in mind, that if you leave crops in the ground for harvesting in the spring, you will need to protect your garden with mulch and be sure to visibly mark where plants are located to avoid accidentally digging them up when you turn your garden over for spring planting. Also, be aware that continuously planting can sometimes exhaust your soil: this can be avoided by continuously feeding your garden rich, organic compost or by giving it a winter break and planting an appropriate cover crop.

Preparing for Spring

The first item on your to-do list before the onslaught of the prime growing season is to have your soil tested.

Here's where you might want a tiller if you have a larger garden. Turning soil breaks up any unwanted roots that may be lurking there as well as aerates the soil and prepares it for planting. Add your compost and organic fertilizer at this time, and be sure that this material is tilled into your garden well before planting.

If the soil in your area isn't conducive for gardening—if it is made up largely of clay, for example—you'll want to create your topsoil layer with organically sourced soil. Depending on how large your plot is, you can purchase gardening soil at many large retail outlets—again, look for organic

—and gardening shops. This can get expensive if you have a lot of ground to cover, so you can also look to local farmers and/or cooperative extension services to find out where you might purchase soil in bulk. You should only need to do this in your first year of gardening, barring some disaster, as the compost you keep should provide you with plenty of healthy new soil to add each year.

This is the time of year that you will typically want to map out your garden space, organizing crops according to some basic rules of seasonality, succession planting, and companion planting, with an eye on the practical logistics of space, weed control, and ease of harvest. Herb plants that you will snip throughout the spring and summer should be easy to access, for example, a long, squat raised bed plot should promote ease of harvesting with all crops.

Certainly, spring is the time of year during which you will do much—if not most—of your planting.

Sustaining Through the Summer

Summer offers up its own challenges, depending on your region. For most of us, the summers will get hot and dry—to what extent is out of our humble control. This is also the season during which weeds and pests will be at their most prominent, typically speaking. It is also a wonderful time of year when your garden will be at its most productive, so prepare for regular harvesting and preserving, if necessary.

Be prepared to visit your garden every day—once in the morning and once in the evening is ideal—to keep up with weeds, pests, and diseases.

Extending Into Fall

The more actively you cultivate your garden, the healthier it will be, and while fall presages the cold nearly dormant time of winter, it can be a lovely time to garden. Pests are fewer, weeds dieback, and diseases tend to dissipate.

Fall is the ideal time to plant any crops that you intend to overwinter, such as garlic, onions, leeks, and various root vegetables or hearty greens. While some of these you will not harvest until the following year (garlic, onions, some root vegetables), you can maximize your harvest by cultivating some fall spinach or other greens to eat through Thanksgiving in certain areas, then cutting the plants back before winter mulching; these will be among the first to poke their green heads up again in spring.

Chapter 20-   Harvesting, Storing and Preserving Vegetables

The quality of your vegetables cannot be improved after harvest. It is, therefore, a must to get your crops at the right maturity.

To retain good quality after harvesting, handle vegetables with care. Preventing it from getting bruised or damaged will not encourage decay.

When to harvest vegetables for the optimum flavor and yield:

- Asparagus: harvest three years after planting. Snap at the soil line, they should be six to eight inches in length, but the heads should not be open. Length of harvest: six weeks.

- Avocados, ripe summer to winter in Florida, fall to spring in California.

- Beans (green and snap): harvest the beans when they are about one-fourth developed; if allowed to develop fully, it will decrease their yield.

- Beans (Lima): harvest when fully developed and beans are green.

- Beets: harvest the bulb when it is 2 inches in diameter.

- Broccoli: Harvest when the head is fully developed, cut six inches below the head.

- Brussels sprouts: harvest them when 1 ½ inch wide by twisting the heads off the stems.

- Cabbage: Harvest when heads are solid but do not allow them to split, cut just beneath the head.

- Carrots: harvest when carrots are no more than one inch in diameter, but smaller is better, as carrots will toughen as they thicken.

- Cauliflower: harvest when heads are full and white.

- Celery: cut celery stems when ten to twelve inches tall.

- Cucumbers: if using cucumbers to make sweet pickles, cut them at 2 inches long, if using cucumbers for dill pickles, cut them at 4 inches maximum, if slicing cucumbers for the dinner table, cut them at 6 inches. Gather daily.

- Eggplant: harvest eggplant fruits when black or purple and firm.
- Lettuce: Harvest the outer leaves at 4 to 6 inches long, leave the inner leaves for more yield.
- Okra: ripe and ready to pick at three inches long.
- Onions: depends upon type and variety of onion, harvest storage onions at two inches in diameter and before a hard frost.
- Peas: harvest peas at full development when pods are full and feel tender to the touch.
- Pod peas: like Spring Peas, harvest at half development when peas are small and soft.
- Peanuts: harvest when pods are yellow and before the first frost.
- Pepper (green): harvest when fully ripened firm peppers, and dark green in color.
- Pepper (red): allow to ripen two to three weeks longer after greening, and pull when red or yellow in color.
- Potatoes: Harvest when fully grown at three inches or more; for new potatoes, harvest whenever ready to eat after one inch in diameter.
- Pumpkins: harvest when pumpkin is fully orange, and skin is hard to the touch.
- Radishes (American): harvest radishes at one to one and a half inches around.
- Rhubarb: harvest after the second year of planting, pull at the root to one side and cut.
- Rutabaga or turnips: harvest after ripe and when the bulb is two to three inches in diameter.
- Spinach: harvest the leaves at no more than 4 inches. They will grow more leaves as long as the root is intact.
- Squash (summer): harvest at 4 inches when the skin is ripe.
- Squash (winter): harvest when the outer skin is hard and not easily

marred with a fingernail.

- Sweet corn: harvest when kernels are filled with milk, silks will be brown.

- Sweet potato: harvest when the sweet potato is 4 inches in length, harvest before the frost.

- Tomatoes: pick tomatoes when red and firm.

Canning Vegetables

Canning refers to the process of packing into glass jars and then heating the jars to kill the organisms that would create spoilage. You can take it a step further by creating all sorts of delicious sauces, jams and ferments, often increasing the nutritional value of your food.

It is also one of the most time consuming and trickiest and requires the largest amount of equipment, but has the major benefit of not requiring the finished product to be refrigerated. If done correctly, you can store these preserves for extended periods in a cool dark place.

Canning is quite a detailed process, so I encourage you to do more research on this topic, but here are the basics:

- Most vegetables are low in acid, therefore they need to be processed in a steam-pressure canner at the appropriate pressure at 240° F. The pressure if you are living at sea level is at 10 lbs. In contrast, those living in elevated areas need to add half lbs. of pressure for every 1,000 ft. above sea level. This is important as you need heat to the vegetables to a level that will kill the bacteria that causes botulism (a serious form of food poisoning caused by consumption of preserved food that is contaminated with harmful organisms).

- All vegetables should be washed thoroughly, and they shouldn't be left to soak as they may

- It is recommended to use jars that are specially designed for home canning, for example:

Dehydrating Vegetables

The key to drying vegetables is through removing their moisture as fast as possible at a temperature that will not affect the flavor, texture, and even color of the food. There should be enough heat to draw out moisture without cooking the vegetable.

Some of the benefits of dehydrating include:

- Great snacks for travel, camping and hiking
- A healthy option for kids snacks
- They take about less storage space
- They won't spoil as the shelf life is unlimited
- Economical
- Quick and easy to prepare
- The fiber content of fruits and vegetables remains relatively the same after dehydrating

Some of the most common and easiest fruits and vegetables to dehydrate are:

- Bell peppers & chili peppers
- Garlic
- Tomatoes
- Onion
- Potatoes
- Mushrooms
- Green beans
- Carrots
- Peas
- Corn

Freezing Vegetables

Freezing is one of the best ways to preserve your harvested vegetables, as they can really last long, with most vegetables maintaining good quality for 12 to 18 months at freezing temperatures.

In freezing vegetables, you must use a suitable container. The ideal ones are the square or rectangular flat-sided containers, as they can fit in nicely in the freezer. Good-quality containers keep the moisture of the vegetable even when in a freezing environment.

Another good option for freezing is using a vacuum seal bag or cryvac machine. They create an airtight seal that will allow you fruits and vegetables to last longer. Oxygen normally breaks down foods, and this problem is eliminated with a good vacuum seal. Besides, this helps to prevent freezer burn.

You can vacuum seal and freeze most fruits and vegetables; just avoid vegetables with high water content such as celery, lettuce and mushrooms (mushrooms are great for drying).

Conclusion

Congratulations! You have reached the end of our book. I hope throughout the course, you have become excited about the unlimited possibilities of vegetable gardening. Here are an edible hobby and pastime that offers you creativity for your expressions as well as food for your table.

All of the information you just read is beneficial to any gardener regardless of age or experience. Now you know just how simple it can be to grow your own edibles in the middle of city living – even if you have no yard or traditional gardening space.

Vegetable planting is going to have a series of ups and downs associated with it. You need to ensure that you keep pushing forward and learning from your mistakes. That way, you end up expanding your knowledge and improving the overall results that you have in the garden. Remember, even experts had to start with very little knowledge in the garden.

There are many secrets to successful vegetable gardening that the novice gardener may want to keep in mind, like must supply soil and nutrients on a routine basis for the plant. Finding the most appropriate way to eliminate pests and diseases, ideally using organic practices.

With these tips, you should find that you are going to be better off in the garden. It is important to keep in mind that for many of these tips, it will help you to plan things out and to consider the layout of your garden in advance.

Perhaps most importantly, it will be important that you do not give up on your first try. While these tips can increase your chances of success in the garden, it does not mean you will have instant success overnight. However, if you keep each tip in mind and use them to help improve the results that you have, in time, you should find that you do end up with a beautiful vegetable garden that you can be proud of.

Within you is the ability to grow a thriving gardener successfully. Make sure you take the time to nurture that individual and do all you can to grow vegetables that you love. With a little fertilizer, quality soil and the right pots as mentioned in these tips, you are going to end up with a garden that you will love, and it will be one that all of your friends talk about for years to come.

Most of all, I hope you have come to understand that you can grow vegetables almost anywhere. Whether you live in a neighborhood where the yards are small or live in a high-rise apartment complex with no yard at all, vegetable gardening offers opportunities to enjoy bountiful produce. It all comes down to knowing about containers, plants, soils, and techniques.

So, what are you waiting for? Apply the knowledge we learned, and exciting results are waiting for you in the world of vegetable gardening. And the best part of all is that you can begin almost any time of the year.